Complete Book of Bass Fishing

Complete Book of

Bass

Fishing

By Grits Gresham

OUTDOOR LIFE · HARPER & ROW · NEW YORK, LONDON

Contents

69-6869

III—THE EQUIPMENT

Complete Book of Bass Fishing

I

THE FISH

Acrobatic leaps, heart-stopping lunges, rod-bending dives—no wonder the bass has such an enormous following all over the country. Here the author battles a 7-pound 6-ounce smallmouth below Wilson Dam, Florence, Alabama.

CHAPTER ONE

The Perfect Fish

Fog swirled slowly upward from the surface of Bayou Courtableu. In the weak light of dawn it mingled with the strands of Spanish moss which hung from trees along the banks to give the beautiful, eerie atmosphere peculiar to southern swamps. I shivered just a bit, and it wasn't entirely from early-morning chill.

Sitting in the front end of the boat, I eased it down the stream in easy spurts, probing the shoreline with the topwater casting plug, catching a bass here and one there. From all directions came the sounds and sights of an awakening wildlife population—an alligator gar rolling for air; an awkward turtle startled from his perch by my lure; bluegills hitting the surface insects back in the brush; a fox squirrel in the swamp scolding a flock of noisy, intruding crows.

But I was oblivious to everything when I finally stopped fishing and sculled along a quiet stretch, at the end of which a huge tree trunk protruded into the water from shore. Some 100 feet before I reached the fallen forest giant, I carefully laid the paddle on the boat seat, got my bearing, and arched the lure toward shore.

The little chunk of wood dropped to the surface beyond a small snag which rose 6 inches above the water, and I let it lie without movement until all was calm again. I freely confess that

I was a bit afraid to twitch it, for it lay in the lion's den. Beneath that small snag was another big fallen tree, completely out of sight except during extreme low water stages. Most anglers knew nothing of its presence and regularly disturbed the spot in their eagerness to fish the obvious tree trunk 100 feet farther down the shoreline. Around this submerged log roamed one of the biggest bass I have ever seen in Louisiana.

I had hooked the fish once. On that occasion I learned about his home when he fouled my plug on the log and tore free, but not before one jump revealed the size of the bass and left me shaking.

Three other times I had gotten this fish's attention. On two of them he stopped before reaching the lure, leaving a washtub-sized swirl where he reversed directions. On the other he struck but wasn't hooked.

I was greedy for this bass, I admit. I was fishing by myself when I discovered him, and never worked that area again unless I was alone. Louisiana isn't noted particularly for big bass, and the state record at that time was about 8 pounds. My bass wouldn't miss that by much, if any, and I wanted him.

The plug I had cast into the spot that morning was a new one, for the fish had never shown interest in the same lure twice. This particular creation, which had come as a sample into the sporting goods store where I worked, floated when at rest but "crawfished" into the depths on the retrieve.

I started that retrieve slowly, with no commotion, but speeded it up once the plug was under water. When I felt the sharp rap of the metal lip of the lure as it hit the log 6 feet down, I kept the reel handle spinning and felt the plug cartwheel over the tree trunk and come free. Then it stopped, and for a brief moment I thought the hooks were hung in the same tree. But they weren't. I had hooked the bass, and I kept him from getting back to the log by putting a lot of my weight on the 15-pound-test line. I horsed him, to put it mildly. The fish abruptly forgot the log and came storming to the surface. With a series of head-shaking leaps he won his freedom. I have no idea what happened, except that the plug came sailing free during one of those wild jumps.

I never saw my bass again, but I have an idea what happened to him. A crappie fisherman caught a big bass in the area not long after

Fishermen test their skill against the wiles of the black bass in large, open lakes . . .

. . . in small, cypress-studded ponds . . .

... and in friendly little creeks.

that. He dunked a live shiner near a snag with a cane pole, and ate the fish in a noontime cookout that same day right there on the bayou bank.

And that's bass fishing!

I don't know many bass fishermen in Arizona or in Florida, in Texas or in Maine who haven't had similar experiences. This is one of the particular delights and attractions of the most popular game fish in the United States.

And the bass is a popular fish, make no mistake about it. It has a dedicated following in virtually every nook and cranny of the nation, many of whom are *exclusively* bass anglers. Bass are found in all of the contiguous forty-eight states, in all of the Canadian provinces, in Mexico, in Puerto Rico and in Cuba. Bass are found in big, open lakes; in blackwater streams and in gin-clear creeks; in sluggish bayous and in swift rivers; in drainage ditches and farm ponds; in swamps and in irrigation canals; in brackish marsh ponds and in the Great Lakes. Tolerant of an extremely wide array of temperatures and water conditions, bass in some variety inhabit a substantial portion of the fresh water of the nation.

Bass are caught by fishermen using a fly rod, casting rod, spinning rod, spincast outfit, cane pole or willow limb. They hit flies, spoons, spinners, plugs, dusters, plastic worms, pork chunks, live minnows, crawfish, worms, shrimp, salamanders and almost anything else that walks, crawls, flies or swims. They can be taken by casting, trolling, drifting or still-fishing. They'll hit day or night, whether it's hot or cold, dry or rainy, windy or calm. And when a bass is on the end of an angler's line, the fight that ensues is spectacular. "Inch for inch and pound for pound the gamest fish that swims."

A veteran bass fisherman knows how to find—and land—the lunkers . . .

. . . but sometimes a beginner wins the day with two small bass on one lure!

That was how Dr. James Alexander Henshall described him in his *Book of the Black Bass*, published in 1881.

Henshall foresaw the future when he wrote, "That he will eventually become the leading game fish of America is my oft-expressed opinion and firm belief." Henshall lived to see this come true, for in the Preface to the 1923 edition of the same book he stated: "There are now more articles of tackle made for its capture than for all other game fishes combined."

There is, however, another facet in the makeup of the black bass which contributes enormously to his popularity. Despite the fact that he can usually be caught on any type of tackle with a staggering variety of natural and artificial lures, there are times when he will not bite at all. There are occasions, and they are not rare, when the expert bass fishermen in superb bass waters, using all of the sophisticated tackle available today, will fail to score. All the conditions may be perfect, yet this intriguing, frustrating and baffling fish will elude the best of anglers with regularity.

Perhaps it is the unpredictable nature of this fish that accounts for the tremendous group of bass fishermen in this country who border on the fanatic. Other species of fish have their particular devotees, but none command such unswerving loyalty as the *Micropterus* clan. The bass is a very personal adversary to these anglers, who will unhesitatingly travel hundreds of miles to deal with a particular bass problem, and do it over and over again. Each time I write of a bass lake or stream that intrigues me, I am flooded with letters from bass fishermen throughout the nation. They want more information, for they plan to fish that particular spot. Distance, time and money are simply obstacles to be overcome in their quest for the golden bass. For these anglers, no part of the fishing process is too insignificant to warrant full-scale investigation. A driving curiosity impels them to read, talk and experiment endlessly in their efforts to master the art. For them, bass fishing is a way of life.

CHAPTER TWO

The Largemouth Bass

THE largemouth bass, *Micropterus salmoides*, varies widely in color depending largely upon the water in which he lives. Generally, however, the fish is dark green on the back and almost white on the belly, with the coloration gradually becoming lighter from back to belly. Along each side is a dark band, less conspicuous in older fish, which is made up of a series of irregular patches. Bass from many lakes—some in Florida are good examples—are almost black in color. On the other hand, those from ponds or lakes which are turbid much of the time are almost white by comparison.

A member of the sunfish family, the largemouth is a spiny-rayed fish with a dorsal fin that is almost divided. The principal species of bass—largemouth, smallmouth and spotted—have three anal spines and usually ten dorsal spines, occasionally nine or eleven.

Since all three species have similar fins and spines, these features are of little help to the angler who wants to identify his catch. Here are the best ways for you to identify a bass you have just taken from the water:

Smallmouth—A series of dark *vertical* bars or stripes along each side, and usually three dark streaks on each side of the head which radiate backward from snout and eye. The entire fish is colored a uniform brownish-green.

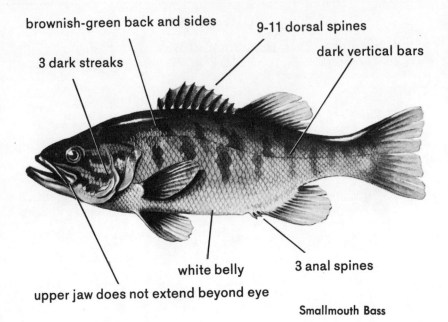

brownish-green back and sides

3 dark streaks

9-11 dorsal spines

dark vertical bars

white belly

3 anal spines

upper jaw does not extend beyond eye

Smallmouth Bass

Spotted Bass— A series of *horizontal* stripes on the lower side of the body on each side. These are the result of dark spots on the scales which are arranged in rows, giving the appearance of stripes.

Largemouth—If neither the vertical bars of the smallmouth nor the horizontal stripes of the spotted bass are present, it is a large-

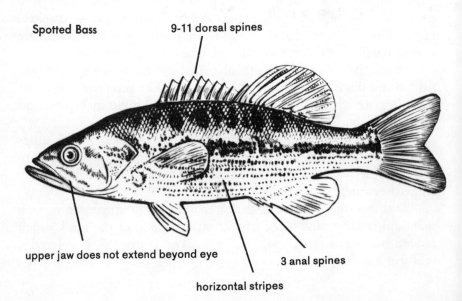

Spotted Bass

9-11 dorsal spines

upper jaw does not extend beyond eye

3 anal spines

horizontal stripes

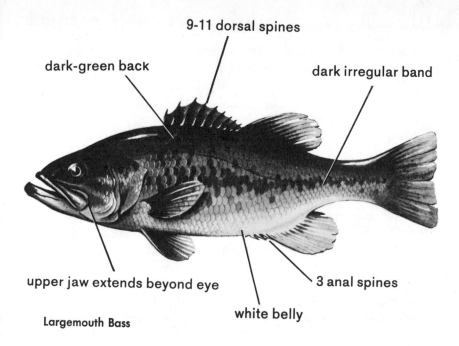

9-11 dorsal spines

dark-green back

dark irregular band

upper jaw extends beyond eye

3 anal spines

white belly

Largemouth Bass

mouth bass. The dark lateral band on each side of the largemouth, from which it gets the name "old linesides," is absent in the smallmouth and much less well defined in the spotted bass.

The length of the upper jaw with respect to the eye is significant. In the largemouth the upper jaw extends beyond the eye. In the smallmouth and spotted bass it does not.

The following overall coloration pattern may be helpful in identifying a bass. As mentioned before, the general coloration of a largemouth is dark olive-green on the back, grading progressively to a pale greenish-white on the belly. Spotted bass, in contrast, have a general appearance of being green on the top half of the body and whitish on the bottom half. It is in this whitish bottom half that the horizontal "stripes" show so conspicuously. Smallmouth bass are called "brownies" in some localities because the fish is an overall greenish-brown with the whitish belly area being very narrow. Again, remember, the sides are usually marked with the vertical bars which may fade and reappear.

Range

The largemouth bass was originally at home only over the eastern half of the United States, but because of its adaptability and popularity the fish has been introduced into many other areas. The largemouth is now found in all of the forty-eight contiguous states, plus Hawaii. It is at home in southern Canada and in Mexico, in Cuba, Puerto Rico and other islands of that area.

Habitat

Lakes, rivers, creeks, ponds, reservoirs, canals, drainage ditches, irrigation ditches, bayous and marshes.

Fresh water or brackish water; clear water or turbid water; still water or running water; weedy water or weed-free water.

That about covers the subject of the largemouth's habitat. The fish is extremely adaptable and is tolerant of a wide variety of aquatic situations. It originally flourished in slow-moving rivers, bayous, ox-bow lakes and marsh ponds. It found a home in the hundreds of man-made lakes which have been built throughout the nation for water supply, flood control, hydro-electric production and irrigation. As a near perfect stocking fish, it is now firmly established in more than two million farm ponds. It has been introduced into natural lakes and streams far out of its original range and has prospered.

Largemouth tend to favor still water and slowly moving streams, but there are times and places where the reverse is true. One such situation occurs in the overflow terrain of the Gulf south when water levels are changing, particularly when flood waters are receding. At these times the greatest concentrations of largemouth bass are found where the current is swiftest—at constrictions as water pours through narrows cuts back into the streams, and on points around which the flow is greatest. However, in a stream which offers a variety of water situations ranging from swift to still, most of the largemouth will be found in the calm pools and eddies.

As for temperatures, largemouth prefer water in the 65- to 75-degree bracket and will seek that strata if it is available. They consume more food in water of this temperature, a fact that has implications for fishermen. They will, on the other hand, tolerate water temperatures higher than 75 degrees, which makes them particularly adapted to life in the shallow lakes and sloughs of the South.

One of the interesting things about the largemouth is its ability to do well in brackish water. This offers the angler a unique opportunity for a mixed creel in some areas, particularly along the coast of Virginia, North Carolina and Louisiana. In those spots it's not rare for a fisherman to take a bass on one cast and a spotted weakfish or channel bass on the next.

Spawning

Largemouth bass spawn once each spring when water temperature reaches a certain level. Some fisheries men say this is about 65 degrees; others put it as high as 74 degrees. There is probably basis in fact for both assertions, but most fish will lay their eggs at 65 to 70 degrees. One Minnesota study revealed spawning two to five days after daily mean water temperature reached and remained above 60 degrees.

The reproductive process of bass is similar to that of all the sunfish. The male largemouth moves into the shallows, from 1½ to 5 feet of water, when water temperatures are still a bit cold for spawning, and begins to build a "nest." This is a circular area in the lake or stream bottom which the bass fans clean of debris and silt. It may be from 12 inches to 3 feet in diameter, and may actually be a small depression.

When water temperature has reached a point suitable for spawning and has remained there for four to six days, the female largemouth moves to the nest and lays her eggs. As they are laid they are fertilized by milt from the male fish. More than one female will sometimes lay eggs in one nest. The eggs are enveloped in a glutinous mass when they are laid, and sink to the bottom where they become glued to rocks, sticks and other debris.

The male bass remains over the nest, guarding the eggs from the many creatures which might eat them. He fans the nest with his tail almost constantly to keep silt from settling on the eggs.

The eggs hatch in from six to twelve days, depending upon the temperature of the water. If the water temperature continues to rise daily during the period, they hatch quickly. If a cold snap occurs the process is slowed.

The number of eggs laid by the female varies widely: as few as 2,000 by a small fish and as many as 35,000 or more by a large one.

Once the eggs have hatched, the swarm of bass fry remains around the nest for a week or so, and the male bass stays there to protect them. After that it's every little bass for himself, since the male turns cannibal and begins to feed on his own offspring.

Feeding

Bass fry begin to feed on minute animal life in the water almost as soon as they are hatched. As they grow, the size of their prey increases, from small insects and small fishes, to larger insects, larger fishes and crawfish.

Once a bass has reached a length of 6 or 8 inches, he will eat almost anything that he can swallow. Anything that runs, swims, crawls or flies is in danger within striking range of a bass.

Bass fry are themselves food for bluegills soon after being hatched, but when they grow a bit the tables are reversed. Then bass become the hunter and the bluegill the quarry.

Crawfish and small fishes of many kinds are the favored foods of an adult bass, but the variety of creatures which have found their way into a largemouth's stomach is astonishing. Included are snakes, frogs, ducklings, turtles, crabs, muskrats, mice and birds of several species.

Bass don't feed constantly—a fact fishermen should consider. All of the factors that influence their feeding habits aren't known, and probably never will be, but we do know some of them.

The erratic feeding behavior of bass has been observed in aquariums time and again. For hours, the largemouth will lounge contentedly in his niche in the glass bowl, paying no attention to the small bluegills and food minnows swiming around within easy reach. Then, as if on signal, the bass will devour the nearest unsuspecting fish. A quick charge—and there is one less bluegill in the aquarium. He will repeat the process several times and then, apparently satisfied, return to his docile role.

Bass usually feed at dawn and at dusk. They frequently go on a feeding bender just before the approach of a storm front. In some situations, with schooling bass, a feeding spree is triggered by the presence of schools of shad near the surface of the lake.

All other factors being normal, bass feed at some time during the day, usually twice, in accordance with the moon phase.

More about several of these factors later in the book, but here let me say that bass need not be feeding for you to catch them; instincts other than hunger will cause them to strike.

Reactions To Temperature

The largemouth bass is apparently most comfortable at a water temperature of about 70 degrees, and therefore will move to find that temperature if it is possible. In general this movement is vertical, from deeper to shallower water, or vice versa. This search for the preferred temperature tends to explain several actions of bass, particularly when we realize that it is not only the temperature of the water itself which affects the bass. The penetrating rays of the sun, for instance, can cause a fish to be uncomfortably hot even when the water temperature is acceptable.

Remember the many times you have been uncomfortably hot while riding in an automobile if the sun shone directly on a part of your body. The temperature of the air inside the car wasn't high, but the direct rays of the sun on your arm or shoulder heated that part beyond comfort. To escape these direct rays of the sun a bass finds cover. He will lie in the shadow of a log, stump, boat dock, lily pad or anything else which casts a shadow. Or he goes deeper. How deep depends upon the clarity of the water, the strength of the sun's rays and their angle to the surface, and the temperature of the water itself.

Keep in mind here that, from spring until fall, the water in most lakes graduates in temperature downward from the surface, which is warmest. Thus a bass may search for the right temperature for his body for two reasons: either to move away from the penetrating rays of the sun, or simply to get into a strata of water which is of a different temperature. The reverse is also true. Bass will move toward the direct rays of the sun, or upward to a water strata which has a higher temperature if that's to their liking.

Fix these principles firmly in mind, for they greatly affect where you will find the fish. By applying a bit of reasoning you can understand the interplay of various factors on bass behavior: cloudy days versus bright days; early morning versus midday; dingy water versus clear water; warming water trends in spring; cooling water trends in the fall; night versus day.

Reactions To Light

It is difficult, if not impossible, to separate the reaction of bass to light from their reaction to temperature. The two are closely connected.

Extreme light intensity seems to have an adverse effect on the feeding behavior of the fish. They don't bite as well on bright days as on dull days. Like most rules about bass fishing, this one is not inflexible. I have caught bass when the sun was bright, and you have too, but that's not generally the case.

The new federal reservoir research program has turned up a rather interesting fact about bass at night. All the fish they have observed thus far seem to be "sleeping." The bass can be approached very closely, then appear startled and confused as if roused from a snooze. Carl Lowrance, inventor and manufacturer of the Fish Lo-K-Tor, doesn't believe the bass are sleeping under these circumstances. He has made extensive scuba observations in connection with the development of the Lo-K-Tor, much of it at night with lights, and Lowrance believes the bass are just blinded by the light.

Sight

Bass have keen eyesight They will frequently move considerable distances while a lure is in the air, meeting it when it hits the water. They will frequently react to the slightest quiver of a topwater lure.

Nobody knows whether or not bass "see" things as we see them, particularly in the matter of colors. Maybe they see a blue as we do, or maybe that blue looks like a red to them. Perhaps they see both as mere shades of black or white. Such a discussion is really academic, for it is true that bass can *distinguish* between various colors as we know them. How bass react to various colors will be discussed in a later chapter.

Reactions To Sound

Bass can "hear" if the noise is in the water. Along the entire lateral line of the fish is a series of nerve endings which act as sensors to pick up the slightest vibrations. This ability of bass to detect and locate objects by their vibrations, quickly and accurately, is of great importance to fishermen. It determines many of the things they should do to catch bass, and quite a few they shouldn't.

Scent

As most fish have a rather keen sense of smell, it is reasonable to assume that bass are fairly well gifted in this quarter. Despite this, I doubt that bass seek their food by scent to any great degree. I think it is significant that bass seldom take dead bait which is just hung in the water. They will take dead bait if it is fished in a lifelike manner, but here sight plays the major role.

Work has been done in recent years which indicates that trout and salmon may react adversely to the scent of humans. A hand dipped into the water upstream has, in some of these studies, caused agitation among the trout downstream. But nothing in my experience indicates that bass react to human odor at all.

Some artificial lures such as soft plastic worms have been impregnated with an artificial odor which the manufacturers claim makes them more palatable to bass. If scent does play a part in making bass artificials more attractive, it would work well with these, for in taking them a bass does so deliberately, chewing on them until he is hooked or lost.

Effects Of Water Fluctuation

Changing water levels affect bass, but their pattern of behavior when the fluctuation occurs is inconsistent and unpredictable. Here are some general observations about how bass react to water fluctuations:

Sudden lowering of a lake after the level has been constant is apt to be followed by poor bass fishing. A classic example of this was provided one fall by Center Hill Lake in Tennessee. Bob Witt, Outdoor Editor of the Nashville *Banner*, and I arrived there to fish with A. J. Hayes, who owns and operates Cove Hollow Resort. Hayes is an extremely good bass fisherman anywhere. On Center Hill, which he knows like a glove, he is deadly. The day we arrived, the lake had dropped some 8 inches, and before we left 30 hours later it was down 20 inches. Before we got into the boat, Hayes said we'd catch no bass, although good strings had been taken the day before. Hayes was right. Three of us caught five bass in two days, most of them too young to know better.

However when floodwaters are receding from overflow areas, the reverse can be true. At such times bass may gather in numbers in some spots and savagely hit a passing lure.

Rising water levels are just as unpredictable. If a torrential rainstorm causes the level of a lake to rise suddenly, bass usually stop hitting. When the rise is gradual, however, fishing is frequently good, as bass move into the new territory made available by the enlarged lake.

Bass As Predators

Largemouth bass, in their predatory habits, resemble members of the cat family, despite the presence of scales on one and fur on the other. Remember the house cat playfully stalking a sparrow on your lawn? He moved slowly and casually until he had a bush between him and the bird; then he began a stalk which was a study in concentration, advancing paw by paw with agonizing slowness until he was within striking range.

I've seen bass follow an almost identical procedure before smashing an insect—or a popping bug—lying on the surface. As the ripples caused by the lure hitting the water disappear, the bass eases nearer, sidling in a circular path until he has the protection of a stick, log, stump or clump of weeds. Next the fish moves directly toward the quarry, pauses briefly once he is in range, then strikes.

Consider, too, a cougar lying on the broad, low limb of a tree, watching a deer approach up a game trail which passes directly beneath. The big cat does not move so much as an eyelash until the buck is in exactly the right position, then he launches himself through the air and has venison for supper. I have watched bass, on many occasions, lie in wait in just such fashion, using for concealment a stump, a weed bed, the piling of a boat dock, a rock or ledge. If the deer passing beneath the cougar is too far away, the cat will usually wait for the next one. But if the deer happens to stop, the cat may make his leap, apparently counting upon the inertia of the standing deer to compensate for the distance being greater than the cougar would prefer. Conversely, sudden movement, a quickening of pace, even flight, will often trigger a cougar's strike.

Bass react in similar fashion while lying in wait for prey. Factors which trigger a bass to strike are nearness of the prey, pauses or sudden flight. The angler's awareness of this aspect of bass behavior is fundamental to fishing success.

Often bass will strike and kill for sheer pleasure. Observe a school of bass feeding on shad. They slash viciously into the school time and again, bouncing them from the water and leaving dead and crippled shad scattered across the surface. It is common to catch a largemouth after such a foray with his stomach full of shad, with shad in his gullet, and with shad in his mouth. This trait is also of interest to the bass fisherman, so we'll keep it in mind, and return to it, as we delve into the subject of outwitting the bass in succeeding chapters.

Small, swiftly moving streams like the Tchefuncte River in Louisiana offer solitude and spotted-bass fishing at its best.

CHAPTER THREE

Smallmouth
and Spotted Bass

THERE are more similarities than differences between the smallmouth, the spotted bass and the largemouth. Many of their characteristics and habits are virtually identical—for example, their catlike tendencies when stalking prey. This is natural, for the three are close relatives. Even their habitats overlap to a substantial extent, and it is not rare in some lakes to catch all three in the same area. It isn't improbable, for that matter, to take the three species on three successive casts at the same spot.

Range

The original range of the smallmouth bass was generally the Great Lakes and the river systems of the St. Lawrence, Upper Mississippi, Tennessee and Ohio. It has been widely introduced now and may be found just about anywhere.

The current range of the smallmouth can be considered to be east of the Rockies, north of the Gulf Coast states and the southern part of Canada. There are no smallmouth in Louisiana or in Florida, for instance. There is some excellent smallmouth fishing in the streams of northern Arkansas and in and below Wilson Lake in northern Alabama. Maine is a state where introduced smallmouth have prospered spectacularly.

Man-made reservoirs have provided excellent habitat for this species, with two of the most noteworthy being Center Hill Lake in Tennessee and Dale Hollow Lake, which straddles the Tennessee-Kentucky border. The current (1965) world-record smallmouth, which weighed 11 pounds 15 ounces, was taken from Dale Hollow.

Lake Erie, in the 19th century, quite possibly had the greatest smallmouth population of all time. According to Trautman's excellent book, *The Fishes of Ohio*, bass were commercially important in Erie from about 1830 until commercial fishing for them was made unlawful in 1902. One report gave the 1885 commercial catch for both black basses, taken from Erie and landed at Ohio ports, at 599,000 pounds. Western Lake Erie still provides excellent small-

Smallmouth bass are able to tolerate colder water than either the largemouth or the spotted bass. This angler has just boated a husky specimen from a lake in Manitoba, Canada.

mouth fishing. Northern Minnesota and southern Ontario are great smallmouth areas.

The range of the spotted bass, also known as Kentucky bass, is more restricted than that of either the largemouth or smallmouth. It extends to central Texas, Oklahoma and Kansas on the west; about midway up into Kansas, Missouri, Illinois, Indiana and Ohio to the north; to western North Carolina, Georgia and Florida on the east; and to the Gulf of Mexico on the south.

Although the spotted bass is best known as a stream fish, it is found in most of the man-made reservoirs within its range, and in many of the natural lakes. Allatoona Lake, in Northwestern Georgia, is a rarity in that 90 percent of the bass taken there are spotted bass.

The world-record spotted bass, an 8 pounder, was taken from Alabama's Lewis Smith Lake in 1966.

In Louisiana, Mississippi and Alabama, particularly, there are many small, fast creeks which are magnificent spotted-bass streams. Floating most of these bears only passing resemblance to the comfortable floats of the Current River in Missouri, or the White or Buffalo Rivers in Arkansas. There are no facilities on most of these little creeks—no boats, boat landings or guides. Fishing them requires frequent pauses to maneuver past a log or fallen tree. These streams offer only solitude and fish.

Habitat

The spotted bass prefers and can tolerate cooler and swifter water than can the largemouth; the smallmouth prefers and can tolerate colder and swifter water than can the spotted bass.

Stream gradient determines where the three species will most frequently be found in flowing waters. Smallmouth prefer a gradient of 4 to 25 feet per mile, while spotted bass like a gradient of less than 3 feet per mile. In streams the largemouth stick to sluggish pools or connected coves.

Strangely enough, the spotted bass is more tolerant of turbid water conditions than are the other two basses.

Smallmouth like a sandy, gravel, rocky bottom in a stream or lake with clear, moving water. They tend to shun weedbeds whereas largemouth bass gravitate to them, but they do like brush.

In reservoirs where all three species are found, the spotted bass will be at the deepest levels—frequently over 100 feet; the large-mouth will be in the next layer above; and the smallmouth will be in still shallower water.

Spawning

Smallmouth begin spawning when water temperatures move from the 50's into the 60's. Although these fish apparently prefer water depths for spawning which are similar to those favored by largemouths, Trautman reported that he observed smallmouth bass eggs hatching at a depth of 22 feet in Whitmore Lake, Michigan. Despite this extreme, all three species of bass normally utilize much shallower water for their spawning. Most spotted-bass nests in Bull Shoals were about 12 feet deep.

In streams, both smallmouth and spotted bass tend to move downstream in the fall, wintering in the deeper pools. As the waters warm up in the spring, they move back upstream and spawn.

The most important cause for failure of smallmouth spawning attempts is abandonment of the nest by the guarding male. When that happens the eggs are quickly eaten by predators. In turn, the most important cause for the male leaving the nest is low tempera-ture. It frequently happens that the water will warm up into the 60's, nesting activities and spawning takes place, and then a cold snap drives temperatures back down into the 50's. When that hap-pens the male will invariably leave the nest and it will fail.

The average smallmouth nest will contain from 2,000 to 10,000 eggs, resulting from one or more than one female spawning in the same nest.

The feeding habits of smallmouth and spotted bass are similar to those of the largemouth, as are their reactions to light, vibration, sound, and water fluctuation.

CHAPTER FOUR

Management

In 1898 the Parish of Orleans in Louisiana hired Robert H. Wilcox to enforce the "green trout" ordinance. That made him Louisiana's first game warden. As I write this in 1966, Mr. Wilcox is in his ninety-third year. He has lived on Lake Hortonia, near Brandon, Vermont, since 1935. When I visited him several years ago he explained the "green trout" ordinance.

"That was an ordinance passed by the Parish which prohibited fishing during the spawning season for black bass. It was my job to see that it was obeyed."

The practice of giving protection to a species during the time of year when it is reproducing is one of the oldest of all the management measures, and it is still one of the most effective for many species in many areas. This is particularly true for most game animals and is true for many game fish.

One of the first attempts to regulate fishing was a law enacted in 1678 by the court of Middlesex County, Virginia, which prohibited the use of jacklights while fishing. Other efforts to protect the brood stock of fish took place in 1734, when the Common Council of New York City passed an ordinance limiting the taking of fish from freshwater ponds to rod, hook and line only; and in 1761 when the General Assembly of Virginia decreed that no man should construct or maintain a mill dam or barrier of sufficient height to prevent fish from ascending spawning streams. Such measures became more numerous in the 19th century, and in the decade from 1870 through 1880 several state fishery commissions were authorized by state legislatures. In 1871 Congress created the United States Commission of Fish and Fisheries.

Creation of these state and federal agencies was followed by an era during which fish stocking was emphasized. It is an important part of the history of bass in this country, for it resulted in a vast extension of the range of the largemouth through artificial introduction into new areas.

Wildlife management is largely a business of manipulating a species of wildlife relative to its habitat, and this itself is in a constant state of change. We are at a period of history when the dangers to the wildlife habitat of the United States have reached alarming proportions. A rapidly growing population calls for more houses, roads, shopping centers and factories, all of which are detrimental to the maintenance of good wildlife habitat. The wildlife manager has an increasingly difficult task, and the management measures which were adequate a decade ago may need revision to cope with present-day conditions.

Closed Seasons And Size Limits

As mentioned previously, one of the earliest bass management techniques was to prohibit fishing during the spawning season. Since the time bass spawn is dependent largely upon the temperature of the water, this closed season varied in different areas of the nation.

Later research indicated that in southern waters the hook-and-line take of bass was insufficient to cause any effect on the year to year breeding population, and most states of the South soon began to permit year-round fishing. This trend spread north and westward, and now many states have dropped that restriction. Other states, generally those in the north where growing seasons are short, continue to use the closed season as a tool of management.

Going hand in hand with the closed season, in most areas, was the minimum size limit. The purpose was to insure that bass grow to "spawning" size before being removed from the water, to insure that reproduction be sufficient to maintain the population.

The size limit disappeared along with the closed season in the states of the South, and others soon followed suit. It was eliminated for the same reason—bass reproduction was found to be ample despite year-round sport fishing for any size fish.

As with the closed season, however, the minimum size limit has been retained by many of the "cold" states. The reason given is that in those areas a bass does not mature sexually until three to five years of age, and the regulations are designed to keep the fish free until it has spawned at least once.

In warm waters of the South and Southwest, most bass spawn the first spring following hatching, when they are about one year old. Under normal conditions, enough young bass are produced each year, even with year-round fishing and no size limit, to more than amply restock these warm-water lakes.

At last check, thirty-four of the forty-nine states which have bass permitted year-round fishing and imposed no minimum size limit. Fifteen maintained closed seasons of varying lengths, and fifteen others—not all the same fifteen which had closed seasons—imposed minimum size limits. Most of the closed seasons, it should be noted, are set primarily with smallmouth bass in mind rather than largé-mouth.

As an indication of the size-age relationship of smallmouth bass at maturity, consider these results of a study made in the Lake Ontario-St. Lawrence River region. The males matured first. Some males matured at the end of the fourth year of life, being about 10.2 inches in length at that time; and nearly all were mature at the end of the sixth year, or 11.9 inches long. Female smallmouth, on the other hand, were beginning to mature at the end of the fifth year (10.9 inches), but not all were mature until about eight or nine years of age, at which time they were 13.7 to 14.4 inches in length. Fish mature earlier in warmer waters where the growing season is longer.

Creel Limits

The third member of the trio of early management restrictions was the creel limit, and this one has persisted in almost every state. In 1962, for instance, only Ohio and Wyoming did not impose a limit on the number of bass an angler could legally take home each day. Creel limits vary widely. Louisiana, for instance, has a daily limit of fifteen. In Wisconsin, it is five largemouth and five small-mouth.

Research has shown that sport fishing for bass cannot deplete the brood stock to the danger point, therefore creel limits must have a purpose other than that of insuring adequate reproduction and maintenance of the species. The purpose is usually described as being twofold: one is to distribute the harvest among more anglers; the other is a psychological one, the theory being that a fisherman is more satisfied when he catches a "limit" of eight bass than he is when he catches twelve bass where the limit is fifteen.

Although I concur that the sport harvest of bass isn't likely to remove enough fish to prevent adequate reproduction, I do believe that heavy fishing pressure on bass can remove—or educate—enough bass to lower the quality of the fishing. There is a decided difference in the two.

Numerous fish pond studies have shown that the quality of fishing necessary to stimulate angling activity disappears long before the bass population is damaged from a standpoint of maximum reproduction. At the point where bass fishing becomes so poor that anglers stop fishing, there is still ample brood stock left in the water to insure full restocking during the next spawning period.

I believe this is particularly true where streams are concerned, especially for smallmouth bass. Quite frequently a stream receives such favorable publicity that it suffers exceptionally heavy fishing pressure. Such a case is the Buffalo River in Arkansas, where on some stretches there were five times the number of float fishermen in the season of 1965 than during the previous five years combined. In such instances I can only believe that a greatly curtailed creel limit should be imposed.

There is another viewpoint toward creel limits on bass which holds that no creel limit at all has advantages. The angler, so this philosophy maintains, will actually be satisfied with fewer fish if he has no artificial goal—no "limit"—to seek.

Restocking

The reaction to poor fishing once was the immediate assumption that there weren't enough fish in the water, and it was a natural reaction. The "cure," obviously, was to restock the lake or stream. However, the assumption was frequently completely wrong, and the cure only aggravated the situation. This was particularly true where warm-water fish were concerned, frequently bass. The actual cause of poor fishing often was too many fish, not too few. This means there were more than the habitat could care for effectively. The percentage of catchable bass dwindled as a result of the over-population. The fish became stunted through lack of sufficient food. The cure in these instances was to remove some of the bass, not to add more.

In the past few decades, most anglers and fisheries officials have been fairly well indoctrinated with these facts of fish life, so there is no need to belabor the point. It does seem advisable to say that over-population is certainly not always the reason for consistently poor bass fishing. There is no substitute for competent, professional diagnosis.

A shortage of bass, especially in one particular age group, is apt to be the result of a spawning failure—or near failure—one season. These failures can be caused by a number of factors. Let's examine the most common.

Suddenly lowered water temperatures, after most of the bass have spawned, can cause failure. While this colder water would not normally keep the eggs from hatching later on, when proper temperatures for hatching were maintained, it drives the guarding males from the nest into deeper water. When that happens most eggs are eaten by predator fish, especially by bluegills and other bream.

If the level of the lake is suddenly lowered just after bass have spawned, a reproduction failure for that season is probable. The eggs which are left high and dry, of course, are completely lost. Others left in very shallow water are frequently destroyed by wave action. left in very shallow water are frequently destroyed by wave action.

One factor that usually insures against a complete reproductive loss in any one year is that not all bass spawn at the same time. This means that some spawners will usually move in again after a catastrophe has eliminated the first wave of nesting attempts.

Fungus is common in bass nests, both largemouth and smallmouth, and once it begins the entire nest of eggs is lost.

Water fluctuation of the opposite extreme, flooding, can also cause nesting losses. This is particularly true in streams, where flood waters immediately following spawning can destroy nests or cover them with silt and debris.

Hatcheries to produce bass are still maintained by many states and by the federal agency, the Bureau of Sport Fisheries and Wildlife. Almost without exception, however, the fish are used to establish a bass population in newly constructed lakes or ponds, or to re-establish one in lakes, ponds or streams which have been renovated.

Fish Ponds

Several million fish ponds have been built in the United States, largely through the impetus and aid of the United States Soil Conservation Service, and more are being added each year. Far too

Several million farm ponds have added bass water to many regions of the country and have given fisheries technicians the opportunity to experiment with management measures.

When a lake becomes badly out of balance, the cure is to eliminate the entire fish population and start over.

many of these, unfortunately, fail to afford the quality of fishing they're capable of because of poor management.

All state agencies charged with fisheries administration will give competent advice on proper pond management, as will the Soil Conservation Service.

Many states have fish pond publications which are available for the asking. Two excellent federal booklets on the subject are: "Techniques of Fishpond Management," United States Department of Agriculture, Miscellaneous Publication No. 528; and "Managing Farm Fishponds for Bass and Bluegills," United States Department of Agriculture Farmers Bulletin No. 2094.

Reservoirs

Exclusive of the Great Lakes and Alaska (which has no bass), there are more acres of fishing water in the United States in man-made impoundments than there are in natural lakes. More than a third of the nation's anglers now fish in these artificial ponds, and the percentage is increasing with every year that passes.

These big reservoirs—1,200 of them contain one-third of all

the fresh water available for public fishing—have a peculiar and erratic pattern of productivity. For the first few years of life fish production and fishing are tremendous, but then the lake normally goes into a decline. At intervals some reservoirs again become very productive for a period, but this is very uncertain and unpredictable. This erratic productivity has been a concern of fisheries personnel for years, but it became more so in 1962. In that year the Outdoor Recreation Resources Review Commission released a report which predicted that by 1976 the large reservoirs would sustain an 85 percent increase in angling pressure—a jump of 75 million man-days in thirteen years. To maintain fishing success at present levels, this means that warm-water harvest from these reservoirs must be increased 30 percent.

With the aim of finding out how to effect this increase, the Bureau of Sport Fisheries and Wildlife quickly began a National Reservoir Research Program. It has its headquarters at 113 South East Street, Fayetteville, Arkansas, and the current Director is Robert

The new federal reservoir research program is even employing a small submarine for extended observation of fish.

M. Jenkins. Using all of the investigation techniques known, including even a two-man submarine for underwater observations, this program is now studying 640 large U. S. reservoirs. Research teams are conducting intensive study of Bull Shoals and Beaver on the White River, and Oahe, Sharpe, Francis Case and Lewis and Clark on the Missouri. In addition to benefitting from the increased reservoir production which should result from this study, bass fishermen will undoubtedly benefit from the knowledge acquired about the life histories and habits of largemouth, smallmouth and spotted bass.

Repressive Factor

One of the most mysterious and intriguing facets of fisheries management is the belief that the fish themselves, once they reach a certain density in a stable body of water, secrete into the water a substance which inhibits spawning. The existence of this built-in birth-control feature has basis in fact, and it is hoped that the reservoir research program will shed additional light on it.

Much of the work concerning this repressive factor has been done by Dr. H. S. Swingle, of the Agricultural Experimental Station, Auburn University, Auburn, Alabama. In 1956 he presented a paper at the North American Wildlife Conference entitled "Determination of Balance in Fish Ponds." Selected quotes from this paper give an indication of the scope of this phenomenon.

The apparent excretion of a hormone-like repressive factor that prevented reproduction was first observed in goldfish, carp and buffalo populations. When these fishes were stocked in ponds several months prior to the spawning period, reproduction did not occur when the water temperature rose to the normal spawning temperature. However, upon transfer of these fish into adjacent ponds filled with fresh water, spawning usually occurred within 24 hours. When the water in which a goldfish population had been kept for several months was pumped into adjacent ponds, brood goldfish in these ponds failed to spawn until this water was completely drained and the pond refilled with fresh water. Heavy spawning of many species at periods of rising water in the spring is probably related to this factor.

It was suspected that the presence of such a repressive factor controlling reproduction was widespread among fishes. There is some indication of its presence in bluegills. ... However, the effect of a repressive factor upon bluegills, if present at all, is insufficient to prevent reproduction before these fish become so crowded that none can grow.

Some evidence exists that reproduction of largemouth bass may be partly controlled or prevented by a repressive factor excreted by bass. After bass have ceased to reproduce in hatchery ponds, additional spawns may often be obtained by transfer of the brood fish into another pond freshly filled with water.

In case of the bluegill, it appears that it may excrete a repressive factor that inhibits spawning of largemouth bass. It was originally thought that the egg-eating habit of crowded bluegills was alone responsible for the failure of largemouth to reproduce in unbalanced populations. However, it was later found that crowding of bluegills also prevented largemouth from laying eggs. Here was a condition in which bass were not crowded, were growing at a rapid rate, but still could not reproduce because of overcrowded bluegills . . . This is a problem much in need of investigation.

Management of a bass fishery is not the simplest thing in the world, but professional fisheries men have made giant strides in the past two decades toward finding out just what makes our favorite fish tick. You have had a hand in their work, since 10 percent of the cost of your fishing tackle goes into fisheries work via the Dingell-Johnson program.

Prospects for the future are bright. Not only are state and federal agencies acquiring better-trained personnel and a constantly expanding backlog of management knowledge, but private organizations such as the excellent Sport Fishing Institute (719–13th Street N.W., Washington, D.C.), which has as its slogan "To Help Shorten the Time Between Bites," are doing just that. Throughout the nation there is also a new and heartening awareness of the necessity to prevent new sources of pollution and to clean up the old ones.

II

THE TECHNIQUES

CHAPTER FIVE

Finding the Fish

THE most important skill for a bass fisherman to master is the ability to find the fish. That is the opinion of the majority of the top-notch bass fishermen I know. This assumes that the mechanics of fishing are under control, that the angler has the equipment and the ability to use it, and that he is fishing in a lake or stream which has an adequate bass population.

The advice to "find the fish" may sound facetious to many anglers, particularly to novice bass fishermen. Their reaction is understandable, for I can remember when I harbored a good deal of skepticism toward the idea. I was living in Baton Rouge, Louisiana, at the time, and considered myself a pretty fair bass fisherman. In that city lived Bill Adcock, who had a reputation as a bass man, and I wanted to see him in action. So we started out one mid-morning for one of Bill's favorite spots in a small lake known as the Stump Hole.

"I feel like an idiot," I grumbled, "starting out so late. Daybreak is the time for bass. Why the middle of the morning?"

Bill merely grinned as we wound our way in and out of the protruding cypress butts that gave the Stump Hole its name. Finally we stopped, about in the middle of the lake.

"That ought to do it," he said. "I've got this anchor down and you do the same with yours. And don't bump the boat. This is where we're going to fish."

To be fair, it wasn't exactly in the middle of the lake. We were probably 50 yards closer to one shoreline than the other but not less than 200 yards from either. To think about fishing out here was bad enough, but anchoring . . . well, that was more than I could bear.

"If I'm going to fish in the middle of the day, at least get me within chunking distance of the bank," I grumbled.

Ignoring me, Bill tied a small, yellow sinking lure to his leader and sailed a long cast out into nowhere. He waited until his plug sank to the bottom, then stuck his 6-foot casting rod into the water until just the reel was clear. Then he cranked in line as fast as possible. A sharp jerk on the rod when the plug was halfway back told me we were in business. Bill eased back on the boat seat and brought the rod up for air just as a 3-pound bass burst through the surface some 20 feet out.

"They're here," Bill said happily. "I was afraid we might not find 'em this easy. Just string this baby and don't let him flop against the bottom of the boat."

"How'd you know that fish was there?" I asked.

"Because he's been there most of the time. Bass don't spend much time along the shoreline," he explained. "Oh, maybe some of the little fellows will move in for a while early in the morning and late in the afternoon. But generally most of the bass are out in the lake in such spots as this, all bunched up like grapes just waiting to be picked."

"There's more where you caught that one?" I scoffed.

He proved it, stringing four bass on the next five casts.

"I know of four or five other spots in the lake like this one, all good," he went on. "Course, you don't hit the fish on each one every time, but by making the rounds I usually get enough to eat."

I could believe it, since we took two-dozen bass from that one spot, moving on only because I wanted to see some of the others.

Now, such an experience would normally make someone think. But not a bass fisherman. I went back to my shoreline pitching. Sometimes—rarely—I would take a limit of fifteen fish, but most of the time a half dozen would be a good catch.

Bill Adcock, of Baton Rouge, Louisiana, who gave the author his first lesson in finding the fish, thrusts his rod into the water to probe the bottom of the Stump Hole with a deep-running lure.

Several years and a couple of hundred miles elapsed before my standard theories were undermined again. I was making my first trip out on Black Lake, a beautiful 20,000-acre cypress-studded water in northern Louisiana. My host was Vic Myers, manager of Black Lake Lodge, and again I ran into a mid-morning start. Vic was busy with his other guests, and he didn't seem to think much of early starts anyway.

I itched with impatience as Vic lingered over a few last-minute chores. Finally, he picked up his rod and tackle box from a corner. The sun was over the tops of the moss-shrouded cypress trees when he headed the outboard boat from the pier into the water wilderness, a fishy-looking forest that had to have a bass hidden behind each tree.

But we didn't stop when we got into the trees. We rode on and on, bouncing off underwater stumps and skidding over logs, for fully twenty minutes before Vic cut the motor. The trees looked exactly like those within a hundred yards of camp, and there was nothing else to distinguish this particular spot from a thousand others we'd passed.

Here's indisputable proof that the Adcock method works. These bass were all huddled on the bottom far from shore. Once he found their sanctuary, Adcock took them on successive casts.

"Been a good bunch of bass using right here," Vic remarked as he began to rig his tackle. "We've taken several limits this week."

I glanced around incredulously. We had drifted into a small clearing of glassy-smooth water. Upside-down cypress trees reached far down beneath the boat, crowned by puffy white clouds that were mirrored perfectly in the black water. If there had been a bunch of bass here, there was no evidence of it now. Vic must have read my thoughts.

"You can try something down on the bottom if you want to—a bucktail or spoon," he said. "Cast over to the edge of the opening and bounce it off the bottom. But I don't think they'll do much with it. They should come up before long and a stick will kill them then."

"You really think some bass are going to break water here?" I couldn't keep the skepticism out of my voice. "Here, and not in those other acres we passed coming in?"

"Oh, we passed up some pretty good schooling spots, but this one has been hot lately. Yep, I expect we'll see some activity before long. If not, we'll move."

There it was again! If the fish didn't cooperate we would move. Why? Obviously, to *find the fish.*

I tried a spoon and then a bucktail with no success, while Vic leaned back against the motor and smoked a cigarette.

"Watch it!" Vic's sharp eyes had spotted the frantic skipping of a shad even before the pursuing bass broke water.

Abruptly, before I knew what was happening, half of that calm, placid pool was a churning froth of feeding black bass. Vic dropped his lure in front of one and was hooked up immediately. He landed that one and another while I struggled with a backlash, an understandable result of my first sight of a hundred frenzied, feeding bass within casting distance.

These anglers are working an underwater reef far from shore. The presence of the reef is indicated by the tips of the trees protruding above the water. When they die and disappear, the reef will be harder to find—but the bass will still be there.

With equal suddenness, all was calm again. Gone were the fish, except for the two flopping in the bottom of the boat.

"That's fantastic!" I said weakly. "You knew those fish were here? And they're not everywhere in the lake like that? No, they couldn't be."

"They're not everywhere, by a long shot. If you don't know where to fish, you can work these trees all day and not get a strike. At times, especially in the spring," Vic went on, "you can catch fish by working the shoreline, but most of them gang up out in deeper water most of the time."

We toured Vic's other favorite spots, skipping vast areas in between, and had our limit of thirty by noon.

One day not long after that, to satisfy my curiosity, I fished Black Lake by myself. I stopped at random out in the lake and began fishing. In one fishy-looking spot or another I fished all day long. I caught one bass. In common with most stubborn bass anglers, I had ignored the lessons that Bill Adcock and Vic Myers had administered. Two years later I got the treatment again.

Buck Perry was the doctor this time. A former engineering instructor at North Carolina State, he turned to the manufacture of fishing tackle for a living. Why, he had asked himself, do bass usually bite "yesterday" and "next week"—but never today?

"The answer is that they don't hit just yesterday and tomorrow," Buck told me. "Trouble was, in the old days I wasn't fishing anywhere close to a bass."

There it was again—the folly of fishing where there are no fish.

"Bass migrate," Buck went on. "Most of the time that you're working that shoreline you don't have any fish to work on. There just aren't any bass there, with the occasional exception of a straggler. The fish which 'use' that stretch of shore are out in deep water, concentrated in an area that might not be bigger than your kitchen floor. Once or twice a day they may move in and fan out along the shore. If you're there when the bass get there, you say, 'They started hitting.' Fifteen or thirty minutes later you find they've stopped hitting. But they didn't start or stop—they just hadn't been there before and they weren't there afterwards. All the rest of your fishing time, except for that half hour, might just as well have been spent in your bathtub."

I was skeptical and my face obviously showed it.

"Come on—I'll demonstrate," Buck offered, and he did. In a couple of hours on Lake Hamilton—we were in Hot Springs, Arkansas, at the time—he *found the fish* and we caught some. Under extremely unfavorable weather conditions, which included a falling barometer and a cold driving rain, fishing in a lake neither of us had ever been on before, Buck located a *group of bass* on the bottom far from shore.

Bass concentrate in particular spots year after year. These fishermen are on a schooling spot which has produced regularly, yet it is not markedly different from other spots nearby. The trick is to find such spots and then stay with them.

The pieces finally fell into place. "All bunched up like grapes, waiting to be picked," was the way Adcock had put it.

"Most of them gang up out in deep water most of the time," Vic Myers had said.

"Bass spend most of their lives in deep-water sanctuaries," was Buck's opinion.

For years I had been fishing in the wrong places. Odds are great that you have too.

In each of the following four chapters there will be information on how to find the fish. As you read, the pieces will, hopefully, fall into place, for bass fishing is not unlike a jigsaw puzzle. It is made up of many interlocking parts, all of which must be present and fitted to make the whole.

CHAPTER SIX

Know Your Waters

ONE of the key factors in "finding the fish" is a detailed knowledge of the water you are fishing. Conversely, lack of that knowledge can frequently prevent you from finding bass, particularly if you have only a limited time to fish.

You've probably heard the old saying that an expert bass fisherman is one who fishes in his backyard lake. By virtue of having covered that water over and over, he usually gets to know it intimately, and his fishing improves.

Bill Adcock went directly to that spot in the middle of the Stump Hole because he knew what the bottom of that pond was like. He had an unusual opportunity to know it, true, for he had been in charge of the crew which had dug it. The Stump Hole is nothing more than a "borrow pit" from which dirt was dug to construct a highway fill. Bill had anchored us within casting distance of an underwater roadbed over which trucks had hauled the dirt out, a roadbed which was from 5 to 10 feet nearer the surface than was the surrounding bottom. He knew from experience that bass congregated at just that point on the roadbed.

Vic Myers passed up thousands of acres of fishing water to take us to one particular spot because he knew from experience it was a hot one.

Finding the fish, then, frequently boils down to finding a place in the lake which has previously proved successful. Often the first hotspot tried won't produce. I have fished half a dozen or more pet holes without success, then filled the stringer on the next one.

In Vic's case, he was lucky and found the bass at the first stop, and in several other schooling spots. Had we not, however, after several fruitless tries, Vic would have altered his tactics and tried different types of habitat. He knows each of these areas intimately. He knows that each represents a different *type* of habitat, and he systematically gives each an opportunity to produce until one does. When one is productive, he knows other spots which afford the same types of conditions.

On most bass lakes throughout the nation there are a few expert fishermen who concentrate their efforts on one particular pond and master it as well as any bass lake can be mastered. On each of these lakes there are other fishermen who fish just as much, perhaps more, but who never get to know the water. They perform the mechanical functions of going to the lake, of casting and trolling, yet they are completely oblivious of the physical characteristics of the water they are fishing. They fish by rote.

The configuration and composition of the bottom of a lake influence where bass will be found at various times, and thus the task of the newcomer on a lake is to learn something of those factors in the shortest period of time. That some anglers are able to do this is proof positive that it can be done. Good maps of a lake are extremely helpful. By examining them at home a fisherman can learn something about the underwater conditions before he arrives at the lake. Then, by supplementing the information derived from the map with an on-the-scene appraisal, he can get a pretty good idea of the underwater picture.

The terrain surrounding the lake often is strongly indicative of the underwater terrain, but this is overlooked by many anglers. If you can get a hydrographic map of your lake, so much the better. This one shows the underwater contours, enabling you to pinpoint reefs, underwater islands, points, ridges, holes and drop-offs. A few states—Minnesota is an example—do fishermen a real service by making these detailed maps available.

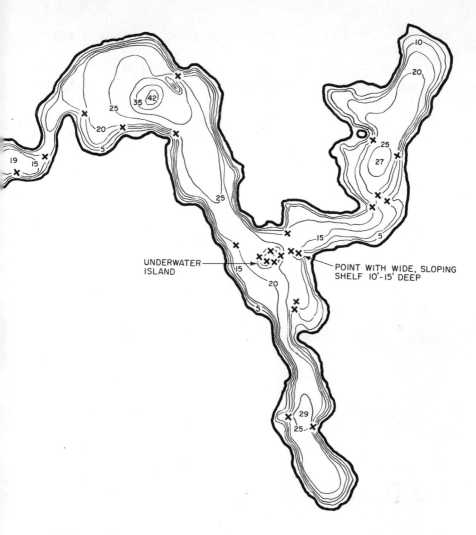

Figures on map:
10
20
42 35 25
25
20
5
19 15
25
25
27
15
5
UNDERWATER ISLAND
15
20
POINT WITH WIDE, SLOPING SHELF 10'-15' DEEP
5
29
25

Hydrographic map is a valuable aid in learning about the bottom of a lake you intend to fish. This sample map is marked with X's to show likely bass concentration points. Most are at a depth of 10 to 20 feet along a bar which extends out from shore. Some of the bars are matched by a point of land extending into the lake, but some are not. Also, some of the bars bend off in a different direction under water from the point of land. A hotspot on this lake is apt to be at the cluster of X's. The long point extending from the east bank has a wide, sloping shelf running from 10 to 15 feet in depth, then a rather abrupt drop-off to 20 feet. The underwater island which rises to a depth of only 10 feet is immediately opposite this point, giving a fairly shallow bench with immediate access to the deepest water around.

You should be beginning to see that the part of a lake we are most interested in knowing—intimately—is the *bottom*. There are several methods of examining that bottom. In clear, shallow water you can see it, but that's of limited value since a major part of the lake is deeper than that. You could use a scuba outfit, again in clear water, but that isn't practical for most of us. You could take soundings, but that is a slow, laborious task which tells depth but nothing else. Trolling a deep-running lure is of value. In the hands of a competent fisherman a bottom-digging plug indicates depth, and also tells something of the character of the bottom—whether it is sand, rock or mud. With a trolled lure you can "map" an area

An electronic depth finder like the Fish Lo-K-Tor is one of the best ways to search a lake bottom for drop-offs, weedbeds, brush piles and treetops, and to follow the direction taken by underwater bars.

Anglers should observe lakes in their low periods and note the types of bottoms in various areas. Low water level on this lake reveals a rock-ledge bottom near the shoreline—a sure sign of bass once the lake rises.

fairly rapidly, and you have an added advantage: you're fishing at the same time.

A fair job of bottom reading by trolling can be done by using a regular bait casting or spinning rig which has some backbone, but only in water down to 10 or 15 feet. Beyond that, and for much better results in the shallows as well, use a short, stiff trolling rod with a heavy, stiff monofilament line. With it you have control of the lure; you have much better "feel" than with a limber rod and flexible, stretchy mono.

By far the greatest aid in reading the bottom, particularly when used in conjunction with a hydrographic map, is an electronic depth finder. One of the best on the market is the Fish Lo-K-Tor, produced by Lowrance Electronics, 7809 East Admiral Place, Tulsa, Oklahoma. With the depth finder you can discover the "breaks" in an underwater structure, such as an abrupt drop-off on a sloping ridge. You can follow much more accurately the directions taken by underwater bars, reefs and ridges. You can find underwater weed beds, brush piles and treetops. The electronic depth finder is not an inexpensive piece of equipment (the Fish Lo-K-Tor costs about $150), but on the big, deep lakes of this nation—and a majority of the reservoirs which have been and are being built fit that description—it ranks in importance with a serious bass angler's outboard motor.

CHAPTER SEVEN

Establishing
the Pattern

It had been a tough day. My fishing partner and I had thrashed Lake Mead from end to end. At daybreak we were drifting popping bugs along the edge of a favorite cove three miles upstream from Temple Bar Landing, and at dusk we were combing another pocket ten miles in the other direction. In between, except for an hour out for a bankside lunch and a snooze, we gave the rods a continuous workout.

Despite the effort, when I nosed the boat up on the gravel at Temple Bar after dark we had only half a dozen bass in the box. We had caught that many more that were too small to keep, and the biggest we had might crowd 3 pounds.

The action, such as it was, was spread thin throughout that long spring day. We would catch a fish in one spot and think that we had found them, then go strikeless for an hour. Off a point, we dredged two keepers up from 20 feet of water shortly after we dropped anchor, but then the faucet was shut. We could not establish a pattern. Most anglers don't, and that is a major reason why their strings are meager. When they do catch a bass they know what lure was on the line at the time—but that's about all.

To "establish a pattern" means experimenting with every variable at your disposal when you begin fishing in an effort to find the combination which will catch fish. There are times when many combinations are successful, but they are rare. More frequently, bass can be caught in numbers only when you meet a particular set of standards and stay with them.

What variables are we talking about? Water depth, bottom characteristics, lee or windward shore, water clarity, vegetative cover. Type of lure, color, size, action, speed and depth. Some of these are built-in, and others are a consequence of the way you manipulate the lure.

For example, everybody has had the experience of fishing on a day when bass preferred a yellow surface lure with spinners fore and aft. But there were other factors in that successful combination. Bass wanted that yellow surface lure with spinners fore and aft, but they also wanted it presented in a certain manner, fished in a certain depth of water over a particular kind of bottom formation, and retrieved just so.

Let me illustrate this idea with an actual experience. There was a day on Black Lake when bass would take a spinner-skirt lure pulled very slowly past cypress trees standing in about 4 feet of water. The lure had to pass within 3 or 4 inches of the tree trunk, and a cast on the shady side of the tree was ten times as apt to produce a strike as one on the sunny side. When we discovered that fact, when we established that pattern, we continued to cast near cypress trees in 4 feet of water; we cast on the shady side and pulled the lure slowly past, just scraping the tree trunk, and we continued to use a spinner lure with a black and white skirt. We caught a bundle of bass.

In the deep impoundments which now furnish so much of our bass angling, the fish often will be found on the bottom at a particular depth, and they will hit a particular lure of a particular color fished a certain way. When that combination is discovered, the obvious road to success is to repeat it until it no longer produces.

Establishing the pattern, then, consists of experimenting and interpreting. The first is virtually worthless without the second. If the angler does not know what he is doing when he does catch a fish, then his success is apt to be short-lived. In that unhappy event his experimenting must be repeated until he again stumbles upon the right formula.

Almost every bass fisherman lies in bed the night before a fishing trip and mentally places himself in a particular spot on the lake he is planning to fish, casting a particular lure. That's fine, except that frequently he continues to fish just that kind of location and that type of lure most of the next day, regardless of what he catches. He should go further and say to himself: "I'll work the shallow cove areas early, with shallow runners, topwater and bottom bumpers. Then I'll move to the channel and check some schooling spots, alternating topwater and bottom scratchers. After that I'll fish the points, and then the creek mouths." If he finds the fish enroute, he should seek other, similar locations.

Experience—real experience—will usually indicate what type of habitat and what kinds of lures and presentations you should try from the beginning. In very cold weather, for instance, it is foolish to spend your prime time working a topwater or a shallow-running lure near the shore. You might end up trying that topwater or shallow runner near the bank after you've exhausted other possibilities, but it makes sense to try the most likely combinations first.

Fishing reports—from newspaper columns, fishing buddies or camp operators—are frequently a valuable aid in knowing where to begin. For years a group of my friends fished one lake regularly. They engaged a guide full time, and each of them used him one day a week, passing on to the next information as to where and how and what the bass were taking. They kept up with the fish. Conditions can change from one day to the next (or from morning to afternoon), but these day-to-day reports gave a more promising starting point for experimenting.

I'm sure you've had the experience of being in a boat where one angler catches many more bass than the other, even when both are using identical lures. The first angler may be lucky, but there is almost invariably some other reason for his greater success. It may be the way he casts, where he casts, how he retrieves, or even the way he has the lure attached to his line.

Now, doesn't it make sense to try to "establish a pattern" when you go bass fishing? It's not really complicated. Just go about your experimenting in a systematic manner, and be aware of what you're trying at all times. When you do catch a fish, if you've followed this procedure, you'll know the reasons for success. Then, most important, you can duplicate the technique and catch another.

CHAPTER EIGHT

Bass in Bunches

W<small>HEN</small> a mediocre bass fisherman catches a bass his usual procedure is to move on and continue to fish. When the expert catches a bass he continues to fish—without moving on. One bass may be the key to the mother lode, for bass do come like grapes—in bunches.

"Bass don't school. They aren't school fish." I've heard that many times, and I expect that you have, too. The truth is that bass *do* school. It follows, then, that there must be a great part of every lake which is virtually devoid of bass. This is an important point to remember, because it means that if you fish haphazardly you may be fishing where there are no bass.

There are certain conditions in a lake or stream which cause bass to concentrate. One is current—water flow. This is particularly applicable in the overflow portions of the mid-South and Southeast, where vast swamp areas are periodically covered with flood waters for part of the year. When flood waters begin to recede, bass anglers often find a bonanza. Fish will congregate where the current is swiftest, which will be around points in streams or lakes. Where overflow waters are pouring back into the streams through narrow constrictions, fishing is frequently exceptionally good. This latter condition is called a "runout"—where flood waters are rushing from a lake or basin back into the river through a narrow channel or cut. Bass often concentrate at such openings in unbelievable numbers.

The mouth of an entering stream is often an excellent spot for bass to congregate. An abnormal current entering a lake can be very good, such as a runoff into a lake following a hard rain. Check culverts and ditch openings where water is flowing.

An abrupt change in water conditions can cause bass to concentrate in one area. If part of the lake is muddy, for instance, don't fail to work thoroughly the murky area between the clear and the muddy.

In a lake which doesn't have a lot of cover, any form of hiding place can cause bass to gather. I live on Cane River Lake, which was once part of Red River. It particularly illustrates this point because cover is scarce and the lake is fairly shallow. In the thirty-five-mile length most of the bass are found concentrated in, under and around widely scattered treetops. Some of these protrude above the surface, but many are down below out of sight. The most productive bass technique in Cane River is to go from one treetop to the next, skipping the intervening water which experience has proved to be unproductive. We anchor at each treetop and fish it intensively, frequently catching several bass at a stop.

Any kind of cover, particularly on the lake bottom, is a likely spot to find bass and therefore should be given special attention. It can be an old auto body dumped in the lake, or the pilings of a boat dock.

Bass in numbers will frequently follow schools of bait fish, particularly shad, giving the angler opportunity to catch them in quantity. In a few lakes of north Louisiana, bass frequent regular schooling spots the year-round. Most of the time they will be on the lake bottom, but periodically they move to the surface to feed on shad, churning the water to a froth and providing one of the most exciting spectacles in bass fishing.

CHAPTER NINE

Bottom Bumping

MORE bass—especially more big bass—have been caught in the past decade than ever before in history, and for this delightful situation one thing is largely responsible. Bass fishermen learned to bump the bottom.

As outlined in the previous chapter, bass spend much of their time in concentrations. Most of the time, when they are in those concentrations, they are on the bottom. To fully realize what I mean by being on the bottom, visualize where a piece of pipe would come to rest if it were dropped overboard. It would not, needless to say, remain suspended midway between the surface and the bottom, nor even 2 feet above the bottom. It would be *on* the bottom. And directly on the bottom is where most bass will be found most of the time.

Now, combine the two facts—concentration and bottom hugging—and a most interesting picture of bass behavior emerges. Any angler who does not take this situation into consideration and act accordingly will not catch many bass.

The fisherman who doesn't realize that bass gather in groups will certainly not catch many fish out of any one school. He probably won't catch any, simply because his lure is apt to miss that

small area where the bass are concentrated. If the lure does hit
the spot, he will probably catch only one because he will move on
after boating the bass.

The fisherman who doesn't realize that bass lie directly on the
bottom of the lake much of the time will *rarely* get his lure down
where he has any chance of hitting a concentration. If he is typical
of a vast majority of bass anglers, he will fish a topwater lure and
he will fish lures which will run as deep as 4 to 6 feet.

The necessity to bump the bottom stems from the fact that the
bottom-hugging fish will seldom hit a lure which passes even a
couple of feet above their heads. The lure must pass through the
school of bass.

It is a common belief among anglers that bass will move many
feet to take a lure; therefore, it is difficult for them to comprehend
that there can be dozens, even hundreds, of bass lying on the bottom
which will ignore a lure pulled just feet above them.

Bass will move a considerable distance to take a plug on some
occasions. All fishermen have had the stirring experience, when
fishing a topwater lure in the shallows, of seeing the wake made by
an approaching bass signal a striking run of 10 to 20 feet. And, if
you react as I do, your instinct is to snatch the plug away before the

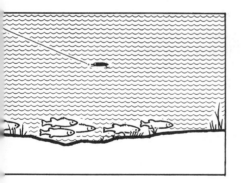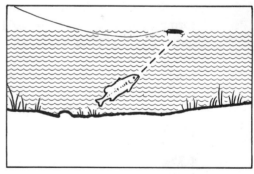

When bass are on the bottom they won't move for a lure pulled over their
heads (left), whereas bass in the shallows will move a considerable distance to
hit a topwater plug (right). This means that the angler must get his lure *on* the
bottom and retrieve it through the school of bass.

bass reaches it. When schooling bass are feeding on shad near the surface, they will sometimes rush to meet a lure before it hits the water, often from many feet away.

But these are the exceptions, since most of the time, in most places, bass aren't in the shallows and bass aren't schooling on top. To be a successful bass fisherman on a consistent basis we must learn to cope with these fish where they spend most of their time—on the bottom, in bunches.

The "bottom" of some lakes, of course, isn't very deep. There are thousands of excellent bass lakes where the average depth is only 5 to 10 feet. In these the bottom-hugging bass are still on the bottom most of the time, but in a substantial portion of them some of those bass are still within range of many bass lures retrieved in routine fashion. This is one of the reasons why southern lakes have such an excellent reputation for bass fishing. With the whole lake of shallow to moderate depth, bass fishermen more often get their lures in range—albeit by accident—than do fishermen working the deeper reservoirs and lakes of other sections of the nation.

Another reason, of course, is that the warm, fertile waters of the South are much more productive of bass than are colder waters farther north. Regardless of their productivity, however, if they were equally as deep it is doubtful that most bass fishermen would fare better than do those who fish in more northerly bodies of water.

You have probably discovered that you catch more bass in the spring than at any other time, if you live where spring fishing is permitted. Why? The answer, and I'm sure you know it by now, is that spring is when bass move into the shallows to spawn. During that brief period the fish have moved up where the average fisherman reaches them with his lures.

Just about any fishing guide, brochure or chamber of commerce promotion will say that bass fishing is best in the spring. For fishermen who don't know what I know about bass, and what you'll know after studying this book, that is true. Fishing *is* best, for them, in the spring. For dedicated bottom-bumpers, however, the spring harvest may be the lightest of all. Because of that spawning movement the normal pattern of bottom-hugging concentrations is disturbed, and the bottom-bumpers find it more difficult to pluck them like grapes.

Not that they don't like spring fishing. Most of them do, and I certainly do. That's the season for topwater fishing, and who doesn't thrill to the smashing strike of a bass mauling a floating lure.

But for the bottom-bumpers the best bass fishing of the year, in terms of numbers and size of fish, is when the fish are not spawning, when they have settled down to their routine of spending most of their time on the bottom.

The importance of bottom-bumping increases, then, as the average depth of the lake increases. For most anglers in the United States the average depth of water available to them has already increased, and more is yet to come.

I speak of artificial reservoirs, for they provide one-third of all the fishing in the nation at this time. Many more—federal, state and private—are slated for the immediate future. Most of these artificial reservoirs are deep. "Deep" is a relative term, but for our purpose any lake which has 12- to 15-foot depths can be so described. Few bass anglers ever work that far down, but that is where most bass usually are.

The older a lake is, the more likely it is that the bass are spending their time in bunches on the bottom. After a lake has settled down following its impoundment, say after five or ten years, the sanctuary resting spots on the lake bottom have become well established.

During the first years in the life of a lake the fishing is best for most anglers. Chapter 20 will explore that at length, so it will suffice here to say that in those early years the bass population is in a state of flux. There are many bass, and they can be taken on the bottom in bunches, but the fish haven't settled down into a fixed routine of which bottom-bumpers can take maximum advantage.

Bass spend most of their time in deep water, in schools, and in a very restricted area—their sanctuary. That sanctuary is most often found in the deepest water of a lake or immediately adjacent to it. It is often on a bar, ridge or reef, a clean spot on the lake bottom. Fish utilizing this hotspot have a regular migration route which they take toward shallow water once or twice a day. This migration route is most often along a ridge, and the sanctuary is most often a fairly level spot—a break—somewhere on that ridge, below 20 feet if the water is that deep.

Concentrations of bass which lie on the bottom in sanctuaries stay in tight groups as they migrate up their ridge path toward the shallows, and they stay on the bottom along this ridge. Not until they reach a depth of 8 to 10 feet do the concentrations begin to break up. From the scatter point the school of bass will fan out toward the shoreline, although the fish may never actually reach shore. On the occasions when conditions are excellent, when the fish do get to the bank, bass fishermen say "the bass are hitting."

You're aware that certain stretches of shoreline on all lakes have a reputation for being good "when the fish are biting," while other stretches are considered poor. Those "good" shorelines are indications that a migration route is nearby and that many bass are huddled on the bottom somewhere along it.

Big bass school in tighter groups than do the yearlings, and they are especially reluctant to move past the scatter point. They seldom do so, in fact, in any numbers. So we return to the premise that we must bump the bottom with our lures if we are to catch many bass, particularly if we are to catch big bass.

Buck Perry, whom we met in Chapter 5, could find no lures which would adequately work the deep water where he was convinced most bass were, so he developed one and has manufactured it since that time. He calls it the Spoonplug, and calls the system of fishing which he evolved "Spoonplugging." His system consists of eliminating the unproductive water. He begins in the shallows and works outward toward deep water, using the appropriate-sized lures for the various depths. In water not more than 10 feet deep, he knows bass could be scattered along the shoreline, for that is within the scatter point. Deeper than 10 feet, he knows bass will be in bunches, on the bottom, usually along a ridge and so he concentrates his fishing there.

Perry usually trolls his lures (where trolling is permitted) to locate bass, since it is a faster method of eliminating the unproductive water. The biggest Spoonplugs, trolled properly, will bump the bottom down to 25 feet, but this is extremely deep water in which to control a lure. Once a concentration of bass is located, the proper procedure is to anchor and cast for the fish. The lure is dropped beyond the school, allowed to sink to the bottom, and "walked"

An assortment of Buck Perry's Spoonplugs for bumping the bottom. Technique is to troll the lure until a concentration of bass is located, then cast and "walk" the lure along the bottom.

back through the bass on the bottom. It is possible to work deeper water by casting this way than by trolling, but it is very difficult. You can get a booklet from Buck Perry on his Spoonplugging method by writing: Buck's Baits, Box 66, Hickory, North Carolina.

About the same time this Carolina ex-teacher was evolving his lure and method, other anglers in scattered locations were beginning to discover bottom-bumping. In Arizona, a close-knit coterie of fishermen began dredging great strings of big bass out of Lake Mead, and from the Salt River lakes above Phoenix. The lures most often used had a heavy lead body, a single hook garnished with a bucktail or rubber skirt, and one or two spinners. But it was how they used them that counted. The accepted technique was to cast close to shore, let the lure sink to the bottom, and retrieve it very slowly with frequent pauses. This allowed the lure to drop from ledge to ledge, or

Spinner-skirt lures are good for ledge-hopping. Cast into shore and retrieve slowly, allowing the lure to slip from ledge to ledge into deeper water (below).

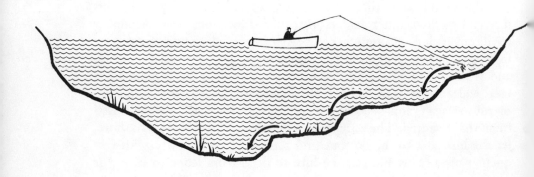

to ease down the slopes where the bottom was fairly smooth. The anglers who mastered this technique discovered that they were most successful some distance offshore from points. What they had done by trial and error was to find the underwater ridges—which extend out from points—and eventually to locate a concentration of bass. They were bottom-bumping. Two other lures which meet the requirement for this type of fishing are spoons and bucktail-type jigs, and they were soon added to the repertoire of the bottom-bumpers.

Then along came the plastic worm. Cotton Cordell, of Hot Springs, Arkansas, developed the weedless leadhead, which enabled anglers to fish the lure on the bottom. Anglers have caught a lot of bass on the plastic worm since it soared to popularity in the mid-fifties. With a variety of rigging arrangements, they got the worms down on the bottom where the fish were.

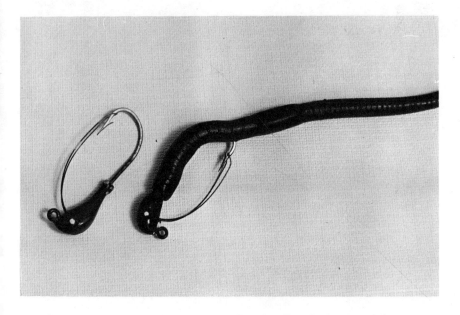

Plastic worm equipped with a weedless leadhead, developed by Cotton Cordell, is an ideal bottom-bumping lure. The worm should be threaded slightly around the bend of the hook so its tail will float upward in the water.

Able to move quietly in relatively shallow water, the wader can reach bass spots he would have to forego with a boat. Belt worn outside waders keeps them from catching on snags and holds the stringer.

CHAPTER TEN

Wading for Bass

For the majority of bass-fishing situations, the best way to find the fish quickly is to use a boat. With a boat you are able to work the deeper water where bass stay most of the time. But for some situations, the advantages of getting on an aquatic footing with your quarry are substantial.

Throughout the nation there are thousands of lakes and hundreds of thousands of farm ponds which have large areas shallow enough to wade. That should suggest that the best time of year to go wading for bass is in the spring when the fish frequent the shallows. Wading is often more effective at such times than fishing from a boat because the angler doesn't frighten the fish as readily. When bass are in shallow water they are skittish, and a boat can startle them. The very bulk of the boat is overwhelming when seen from below in very shallow water. Noise or vibration is much more apt to frighten bass in the shallows than in deep water, and it is very difficult for an angler in a boat to keep from bumping something. If the water contains stumps, trees or bushes, which the shallow areas frequently do, the collision of a boat with these can send bass scurrying for other parts.

A wader, on the other hand, can move very slowly, avoiding

contact with stumps, logs or trees. He has no boat on which to bump his rod, and no tackle box to scrape along the boat bottom. If there is a wind blowing, and that is normally the condition in the spring, the advantage of the wader is even more pronounced. He has no problem controlling a windblown boat. He is relieved of the necessity of grabbing a paddle to keep the boat from bumping into a tree, or from moving past a choice spot before he can fish it.

The wader can work an area *thoroughly*, and there lies one of the chief advantages of wading. He can present his lure to each spot which might harbor a bass and present it time and again to the same spot if he so desires. And he should want to make repeated casts to the same spot. Whether spawning or not, many bass can be irritated into striking a lure by repeatedly pulling it past them. It may be the fifth cast to a particularly good-looking spot, or the tenth, which finally triggers action.

In many areas of the nation late winter and spring rains, coupled with runoff from melting snow packs, send streams and lakes over their banks. Thousands of acres of wooded land are inundated with from 1 to 3 feet of water and bass find a fertile ground for roaming. In this flooded timber a boat is often out of the question because the trees are just too thick. Even where you can maneuver a boat in and around them, wading allows you to fish the area much more thoroughly and effectively.

Bass spread out with overflow waters for several reasons. Food is abundant in the new ground. Advancing water moves earthworms before it, at times producing a staggering concentration of worms at and near the water's edge. Crawfish are on the move as the warmer waters fan out through the timber, and this little crustacean is probably the favorite food of bass. If the time and temperature are right, bass surge into newly flooded ground to spawn. The current itself is another reason and possibly the most important. As water levels fluctuate and water begins to flow swiftly in lakes where little movement is the norm, bass become very active, surging through the overflow in packs, feeding savagely and moving on.

As an example of what kind of fishing you can hope for in some of these overflow situations, consider that a couple of friends of mine caught fifty-seven bass while standing shoulder to shoulder in the same spot. Where you're finding the bass in clusters, there are

Anglers don chest-high, stocking-foot waders and sneakers for a trip into an overflow region where the water may be fairly deep. Waders are also available with boot feet integral with the pants.

advantages to working in pairs. When a fish is hooked the rest of the cluster tends to rally around the struggling bass, often trying to take the lure from his mouth. In that case, the second fisherman has only to drop his plug into the melee for a sure strike. If you hook a bass first, wait until your partner has one on, then bring yours in quickly and string him. With proper timing you and your partner can keep the bunch of bass interested while you thin their ranks appreciably.

Working alone, you'll frequently find that your bunch of bass will move off while you are stringing a fish. Once the attraction of the struggling fish is removed, they may lose interest and wander on. Then you must find them again. Since you aren't nearly as mobile when you are wading, it is important to take full advantage of the situation when you do locate a concentration of fish.

Let me emphasize that wading for bass is effective in all parts

Boats take anglers into an area shallow enough to wade. Inundated wood-lands, caused by rains and spring runoff, provide a food-rich habitat for bass.

of the nation where bass are found. There are still some areas where few bass fishermen wade, but that's because most haven't discovered this pleasant and successful technique.

Wading Gear And Techniques

In wading for bass, use the same fishing tackle which you would use in boat fishing. Of course, you can't troll, nor can you use a fly rod in thick stands of flooded timber.

I prefer to wear an old pair of pants, an old shirt and a pair of sneakers when I wade, with the pants fastened at the cuffs by rubber bands. This outfit is fine for summertime in the South, but in most other areas more protection from the cold is needed. When I need more protection, I prefer chest-high waders, waist-high waders or hip boots. Waders come in two general types. One is the "stocking foot" kind, over which you wear wading shoes, sneakers or some other type of foot protection. The other has the shoe built on. They are made in both insulated and uninsulated models. The kind you select is purely a matter of personal preference. Some waders have a pocket in them, either inside or outside and this is handy. Wear an old belt *outside* your waders. It keeps your waders from "ballooning" out to catch on snags and thorns and it affords a place where you can attach your fish stringer. Carry a landing net if you like.

In most circumstances it is not necessary to carry along a big supply of lures when wading. Half a dozen in a couple of small plastic boxes, carried in a shirt pocket, will usually be enough. You won't be too far from your boat or your shoreline cache to be able to make a return trip if necessary.

Anchoring their boat, anglers begin wading in a brushy area which has been flooded by overflow waters. Fluctuating water levels send bass on a feeding spree.

Anglers should take precautions when wading an unfamiliar lake which may have deep holes. Inflatable fishing vest (above) holds tackle in its numerous pockets, becomes a buoyant life preserver with a few puffs into the valve. The Res-Q-Pak, a pocket-sized life preserver (below), inflates from a CO_2 cartridge with a squeeze of the hand.

Tucker Fish-N-Float, a canvas-covered inner tube with a built-in seat, suspends angler in water and allows him to explore deep areas without a boat.

One other effective piece of equipment is an inner tube which has a canvas seat covering it. In this rig you aren't really "wading," but it gives most of the advantages of wading plus some of boat angling.

Safety

It should be self-evident that a fisherman must check carefully the water he intends to wade, but the warning is worth giving. On several occasions after moving from one area of the lake to another, I have very nearly climbed over the side of the boat into water that was over my head.

No matter how well you know a lake, there is always the possibility that you will step into a hole or a channel. Keep that in mind at all times. If you can't swim and there is any water in your lake that is over your head, wear a "ski" belt while wading. Even if you can swim, additional insurance is worth carrying along. Cold water, swift current and heavy clothes and waders could nullify efforts of even a good swimmer to stay afloat.

One precaution is the Res-Q-Pak, a cigarette-sized life preserver which inflates from a CO_2 cartridge at the squeeze of a hand. It is one of the handiest auxiliary life savers on the market, and can be kept in a tackle box ready for use when needed. When wading, stick it in your shirt pocket and attach the safety clip to your shirt.

Another precaution is an inflatable fishing vest made by Stearns Manufacturing Corporation. It has all of the pockets common to such jackets, yet a few puffs into a handy valve inflates it enough to support a man.

I have itemized some of the advantages of wading for bass, but I've omitted one of the most important. It's fun! There is something about sloshing around in the element of the fish that is exciting and different. I get a big thrill out of having a bass roar past me just feet away after I hook him and I expect you will, too, if you give it a try.

CHAPTER ELEVEN

Night Fishing for Bass

Broken clouds slid across the face of the full moon, casting an ever-changing pattern of grotesque shadows over the scene. During one of the breaks, I zeroed in on the shoreline, then fired the topwater lure toward it in a gentle arc that didn't disturb the water greatly.

With the slight wind drifting our boat, I started the retrieve immediately to keep my line from wrapping around stumps, and geared my reel speed until a satisfying "plop-plop-plop-plop" came from the darkness.

The light of the moon was again diluted by clouds, and the lure was about halfway back to the boat, when the bass hit. There are many descriptions of the sound made by bass taking on top, but the best I can do is to say it reminded me of a dog falling out of the boat.

This fish meant business, but his attempt to swallow the black Jitterbug was only half successful. When the hooks went home the bass went wild. He lunged into the air twice in rapid succession—I could hear but not see—then bored down and out, weaving my line in and out the numerous stumps and snags.

I informed my fishing partner that we must not, at all costs, lose this fish, for it would certainly break the state record of 11 pounds, 11 ounces. With the aid of furious paddling and a 15-pound-test line (with a leader tip testing 40), we managed to boat the bass.

I was convinced that this was a real lunker, but I revised my estimate when I aimed the flashlight beam into the net.

"Not as big as I thought he was," I commented, grabbing him in the mouth and avoiding the treble hooks. "Good fish, though. I figure about 6 pounds, maybe 7."

In the cold light of dawn, on the fishing camp scales, the bass barely topped 4 pounds.

Some fishermen like night fishing; others dislike it very much. There apparently isn't much middle ground. But night fishing *is* different. The lake looks different; the sounds are different; and the bass seem to act different—all because when vision is impaired, as it is at night, the mind is free to conjure up pictures of its own. Like a 12-pound bass.

There are several reasons why bass fishing at night can be both pleasant and productive. Bass move to shallower water at night, where they are more easily worked by fishermen using topwater lures. The sun's rays penetrating clear water can raise the body temperature of a bass to an uncomfortable level, higher than that of the water surrounding him. To avoid that, he moves deeper when the sun is shining. He moves upward to compensate for the heat differential in reverse fashion. The bigger the bass the more affected he is by heat, since his body intercepts more of the sun's rays.

Apart from the question of body temperature, bass seek to avoid high light intensities. The easiest way for them to accomplish this in the daytime is to go deeper and deeper until light penetration decreases sufficiently. At night, however, light intensity is no problem and bass can, if they choose, move right into shore in extremely shallow water. This is one of the reasons why more bass are taken on surface lures at dusk and at daylight, and especially at night.

Boat traffic on heavily used lakes, particularly the smaller ones, can keep bass pushed into deeper water than they would ordinarily utilize. The angler who fishes at random in shallow to moderate-depth water won't catch any fish, and neither will the bottom-bumper, as the fish will be deeper than he can effectively work. Too much boat traffic, particularly from pleasure boaters in fast craft and from water skiers, can make fishing unpleasant. Even where boaters and skiers use utmost care and consideration, if there are enough of them and the lake is small, the angler hasn't got a chance. In this case the solution frequently is to fish at night. Many resort lakes which are thought to be fished out can often yield a full string to the crafty angler who snoozes while the sun is high, then sneaks afloat after dark.

Furthermore during the summer vacation period, daytime temperatures on many lakes are apt to be so high that fishing is unpleasant. Wind also can be a great problem on big lakes, making it dangerous and uncomfortable to be afloat. Most of the time that wind diminishes, or dies, at night. The solution to both these problems is to fish at night.

Safety At Night

Night fishing requires certain safety precautions.

First, of course, make sure that your boat has the proper navigation lights, that they are working, and that your batteries are in good shape.

Take along a flashlight. Don't flash it on the water or against the shoreline often, for it does frighten bass, but use it as need be to locate yourself. Use it guardedly in the boat when changing lures and when unhooking and stringing a fish.

Don't try to land bass at night by grabbing them in the mouth. Because of the poor visibility you're more apt to get a hook buried in your hand.

Use a net if the fish is big. If he feels like a real trophy, use your flashlight to illuminate the netting action. This will probably frighten other bass in the immediate area, but it's worth it if the fish is big enough.

When motoring from one place in the lake to another, don't go as fast as you would in the daytime. If that sounds elementary, so be it, but it is an important point. It's not fun, and can be tragic, to turn a boat over at night. Panic is difficult to avoid when it is too dark to see where the shore is.

Use your flashlight or spotlight to pinpoint landmarks when underway at night, for it is easy to get off course. If you don't need it, however, don't use it. The less you use a light at night the better you can see, which is not as paradoxical as it sounds. It is simply that your eyes become accustomed to darkness after a period of time and compensate to a remarkable extent. One good shot of light can negate quite a period of night adjustment, which is the reason for using that flash sparingly.

At night—and again it sounds paradoxical—you see objects better if you don't look directly at them. This is true because your vision at night is best around the periphery of the retina. If you stare directly at something it tends to fade away. You can see better if you keep your eyes moving slightly around the area you want to see.

Most fishermen, especially those who are good swimmers, don't wear a life jacket or life-preserver belt while in a boat. Most state laws require that you have one, or a preserver cushion, in the boat, but not that you put it on. Put on a life jacket at night if you are running in unfamiliar waters, or running in water where collision with stumps, logs or rocks is likely.

There are a couple of other items of equipment which have considerable merit when considering water safety, and both were mentioned in the previous chapter on wading. They're the Res-Q-Pak, the cigarette-pack size preserver which inflates with a squeeze; and the buoyant or inflatable jacket.

A variety of buoyant coats and jackets are available which are nice looking, comfortable and appropriate for various kinds of weather. As of this writing they have not passed the Coast Guard's life-preserver requirement for boats, but one of these *worn* is more likely to keep you from drowning in an emergency than is an approved jacket which is wedged somewhere under a seat.

The Stearns Manufacturing Company, St. Cloud, Minnesota, makes a line of buoyant jackets and coats. Some have built-in buoyancy; others are inflated with a few puffs when you are in a potentially hazardous situation. Also, Eddie Bauer Outfitters, of Seattle, Washington, offers a buoyant coat which is made in Norway.

Make it a point to carry a compass in your tackle box at all times, especially at night. Darkness has a way of making things look much different, of changing north to south with remarkable ease. Fog is much more likely to form over bodies of water at night than in the daytime, and the combination of fog and darkness can cause you to lose your bearings. You are never lost in such a situation, but it might take five or six hours to pinpoint your exact location. A compass is good insurance to carry with you on night fishing jaunts.

Lures

The only difference I've found between night and day insofar as lures are concerned is that the fast retrieve, which is frequently very effective during daylight hours, usually isn't after dark.

Use the regular assortment at your disposal, with emphasis on topwater, spinner-skirt lures, and bottom-bumpers such as plastic worms and bucktails.

CHAPTER TWELVE

Fishing Natural Baits

THE favorite natural baits for bass are small fish, crawfish, salamanders, frogs, eels and earthworms. Others which are good at times, and excellent in some areas, are grasshoppers, caterpillars, dragon flies, crickets and shrimp.

Methods of capturing live bait are fairly standard throughout the country, but there is one which is new and practical for the angler who has a Fish Lo-K-Tor. He motors across the lake until his dial indicates a school of bait fish just beneath the surface, then drops a basket-like scoop overboard and pulls it through the shiners or shad. The scoop can be made of any small-mesh wire—hardware cloth is good—and the design can be varied to suit personal tastes. One thing is important: Have the scoop tied to the boat with a short length of rope, because there will be substantial drag when it is lowered over the side.

Natural bait is almost invariably more effective if it is alive, and this is particularly true where bass are concerned. Accomplishing this is often difficult in hot weather, but new products and ideas make it possible most of the time.

Minnow buckets are much superior to those available only a decade ago, and many bait dealers now package minnows in small plastic bags injected with oxygen which will keep them in good condition for several days.

Shad, which are excellent bass bait, are very difficult to keep alive. One trick favored by Alabama anglers is to build a redwood box in their boat and fill it with water from the lake or stream where the shad are caught. Don't crowd the fish, and keep the box covered.

Another good method developed by fisheries workers who transfer threadfin shad from one lake to another is to use a tub of some kind (a washtub will do). They place a cake of ice in the center of the tub and put just a few inches of water in it. The shad swim around the block of ice and don't scuff their heads and sides against the tub. Again, keep the tub covered to keep out most light. Wet sacks are handy for this.

Crawfish keep well in a shaded bucket. Cover them with wet moss or weeds.

Earthworms keep extremely well in the new prepared mixes such as Weber's "Mr. Worm." This comes in a dry, 1-pound brick which is mixed with a small amount of water when ready to be used. It provides bedding and food for the worms and is at its best when used in a plastic-foam bucket. Another advantage is that this mix is clean to use.

Technique Of Fishing Natural Bait

Keep in mind that successful use of natural bait for bass sometimes involves as much skill as does the use of artificials. There are times, of course, when any live bait dropped into the water will catch some bass, but there are more periods when careful presentation is essential.

Natural baits are best used with a cane pole, fly rod or spinning rod. The aim should be to get the bait into the water near bass in an unobtrusive manner. Use a cane pole or fly rod for still-fishing, which does *not* mean sitting in the same place all day. It is simply a method of fishing which doesn't call for casting.

In most cases, the least amount of weight you can use the better off you are; and the smallest float that will indicate the action down below, the better. Sometimes it's best to use neither sinker nor float. One of the exceptions to this rule is when fishing in heavy brush. In this case a very heavy sinker placed fairly close to the hook is needed, and is used with a tight line (no float). With this rig you can lower the bait down through the limbs of the brush without fouling the line too often.

With a light-to-medium spinning outfit live bait can be cast into the pockets where bass might be. This is a favorite method of many anglers after smallmouth and spotted bass in streams, where short casts are sufficient. They normally use minnows hooked through the lips, with no sinker or float.

Some of the finest smallmouth in the nation are taken each year below Wilson Dam, at Florence, Alabama, by fishermen using live herring shad (they call them skip-jacks) for bait. They hook the shad through the lips, use no float and only a heavy split-shot sinker, and drift downstream in the swift water.

A spinning rig is excellent for this type of fishing. Leave the bail open and hold the line on your finger, letting the bait drift behind the boat just above the river bottom. When the bass takes the shad, you can immediately release the line so there will be no drag. After the bass has made his first run, engage the bail and strike.

Still-fishing with a fly rod, with live shad for bait, is also an extremely effective big-bass tactic in many areas.

One of the difficulties of fishing with live bait is knowing whether a bass has picked up your bait or whether you've fouled the hook on the bottom or on a limb. This is a predicament that only an educated "feel" can resolve, and then not always. When fishing still water and you feel the line tighten, give it slack. If it moves off it's a fish. If it doesn't move off, it is probably a limb or the bottom.

Live bait which is mobile—shad, shiner, crawfish, salamander—should be allowed to move around in the water whenever possible. This calls for a light line—monofilament is best—with no sinker or float. Some of the biggest bass in the country, the outsized Florida lunkers, are taken on huge shiners which are allowed to swim free. Hook the shiner through the back just forward of the dorsal fin, using a 1/0 or 2/0 hook, and use a float to keep it off the bottom. When Florida fishermen slowly troll these big shiners, another effective method, they hook the bait through both lips.

Live herring shad are a favorite smallmouth bait of anglers who fish below Wilson Dam, Florence, Alabama. They hook the shad through the lips and attach a split shot about a foot up the line (above). Rig for catching the shad consists of a hookless lure with several small flies tied behind (below).

LIVE BAITS AND HOW TO HOOK THEM

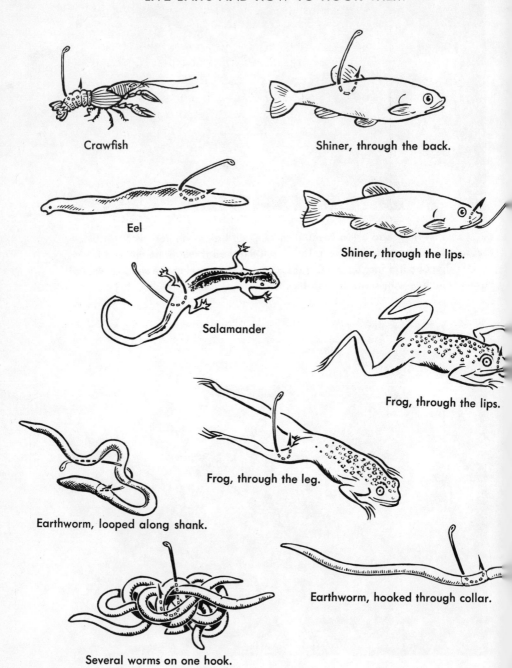

Crawfish

Shiner, through the back.

Eel

Shiner, through the lips.

Salamander

Frog, through the lips.

Earthworm, looped along shank.

Frog, through the leg.

Several worms on one hook.

Earthworm, hooked through collar.

When fishing a live eel, another excellent bait, use a 2/0 or 3/0 hook through the eel just forward of the tail. Cast and let the bait sink to the bottom, then retrieve it in little twitches of your rod. As with shad, and even more so, the bass must be given time to take the eel after he picks it up. A count of ten before setting the hook is generally right.

Crawfish are most effective fished on the bottom, and a bit of weight on the line helps get the bait down. A couple of split-shot sinkers is usually enough. Just cast and let the bait go to the bottom and crawl around down there. The long count before striking isn't as necessary here as it is with the shad or eel. If more weight is needed with crawfish, try the sinkers with a hole through the middle which lets the line run free. After it takes the bait to the bottom, the sinker will stay there and give slack as the crawfish moves around. A pyramid sinker is also effective for this.

Live shrimp are good bass bait in the brackish waters along the coast. Hook them through the tail and fish them as you would a live minnow.

Shrimp keep best when the natural brackish water is allowed to circulate through the container. Some boats have bait wells which permit this, but a minnow bucket tied over the side serves the same purpose.

CHAPTER THIRTEEN

Artificial Lures

THE six most important characteristics of an artificial lure are its action, color, depth, speed, feel and size. Some of these are more important than others, but that order of importance will vary from place to place and from season to season. The essential fact is that all have a bearing on the effectiveness of the lure.

Action

Some lures have built-in action; but others must have it added by the angler. When you buy a plug take time to read the instruction sheet which most manufacturers include with it. Much time and effort went into development of that plug, and it is probable that the maker has discovered the best way to fish it.

Most lures with no action of their own are either topwaters or are designed for bottom-bumping. In both cases a majority of the fishermen using them display a staggering lack of imagination and ingenuity in supplying that action. Experiment with the lure, even those with built-in action, to see if your manipulation can add something. It frequently can.

Color

Bass display color preferences, and those preferences vary from place to place and from time to time. Some anglers believe that color is not as important in surface lures as it is in underwater lures. But as long as color can be of *any* importance at any time, it can mean the difference between catching bass and not catching them.

Depth

If your lure isn't working on the level where most bass are, your catch is apt to be meager, for these fish will seldom move very far either up or down to take a plug. That being the case, it pays the fisherman to know how deep his lure is running, which is not as easy as it might seem. Usually one overestimates the depth one is reaching.

Bottom-bumpers, topwater and shallow-running lures which ripple the surface present no problem of depth control, but considerable experimenting is necessary in order to determine the level at which the intermediate plugs run. The best way is to run a lure in gradually deepening water until you stop bumping bottom with it, and measure the depth right there. If you have a Lo-K-Tor this process is greatly simplified.

A practice which seems obvious, but one that a majority of the bass fishermen never utilize, is to let the lure sink to a predetermined level before beginning the retrieve. By reeling in spurts, and twitching the plug along, it can be kept at the desired level.

Speed

There was a time when the bass fisherman's slogan was that any speed of retrieve was fine as long as it was slow. Fortunately for bass, there are still too many anglers who believe that.

Most lures with a built-in action display their best action at a particular speed of retrieve, so it is axiomatic that fishermen should learn what that speed is. It is easy to learn this by watching the lure as you pull it alongside the boat. Some lures must be retrieved at a slow to medium rate or their action is completely destroyed, and that too can be easily determined. There are others, however, which either require speed or permit it, and with these I have caught far more bass by burning them through the water than I have by letting them loaf.

There are still times and places when a slow retrieve works best. As a general rule I would say that the deeper the fish and the colder the water the slower the lure should be moved.

Feel

Bass can, with the action of their gills, literally inhale a bait, and they can just as easily exhale, or eject it. How it "feels" to them largely determines how long they will mouth it before either accepting or rejecting it. When they hit a hard lure—wood, metal or plastic—they will eject it immediately unless they are hooked.

The first effective soft lure was the pork rind or pork chunk, which is really a halfway house between natural bait and artificials. Then came plastic worms and eels, with such a lifelike feel that bass actually mouth them around and finally swallow them as they would an edible bait. And, more recently, have come soft plugs, both topwater and underwater. They are made of soft plastics by Burke-Flexo, and the company maintains that bass will hang on longer before rejecting them than is the case with hard lures, giving the angler a better chance of hooking the fish.

Size

The size of a lure can play a decisive role in catching bass. This is not a question of matching the size of the bait with the size of the bass, for it is common for very small fish to strike lures almost as big as they are. Size is important for two reasons: Either the lure matches the size of a particular forage fish the bass are feeding on, or it is so different in size from the abundant forage fish as to attract the attention of bass. The other is the surface disturbance created by the lure when it hits the water. On occasions when bass are skittish, usually in very shallow water, a small lure which makes little noise on landing may be more effective than a big, noisy plug. On other occasions the reverse could be true—the noisy landing of the lure is necessary to arouse the attention of the bass.

Bass And Fly Fishing

Artificial flies were the first lures used for bass, since fly fishing predates plug casting, spinning and spincasting by many years. Artificial flies and fly fishing, in fact, date back at least to the ancient Greeks and Romans.

One of the first artificials used in this country was the "bob," which originated in Florida more than two hundred years ago, and which was described by the naturalist Bertram, in 1764, as follows: "The 'bob' is composed of a triple hook, or three hooks tied back to back, and invested with a portion of deer's tail, in the manner of a large, bushy hackle; often intermixed with red and white feathers or strips of scarlet cloth."

Does the lure sound familiar? It describes pretty well today's jigs or bucktails.

The first bass artificials were flies. Next came the fly and spinner combination, and then the bass bugs. Some of the popular early fly patterns for bass were the Miller, the Oriole, the Polka, the Henshall, the La Belle, the Silver Doctor and the Professor.

Streamer flies, which are fished wet, are very effective on bass, and that effectiveness was increased when John Hildebrandt, an excellent Indiana fly fisherman, produced a spinner small enough to be used in front of it. The Hildebrandt name is still associated with spinners, for it is a leading tackle manufacturer today.

Most fly fishing for bass today is done with bass bugs, which were an American concoction. Dr. James Henshall, in his *Book of the Black Bass*, dismissed bass-bug fishing as falling far short of fly fishing in its best sense. The first bass bugs he had seen were sent to him by Mr. M. D. Butler, of Indianapolis, Indiana, in 1893, and Henshall described them as "made with plump, buoyant bodies, dressed with silk floss and feathers, and with long wings, hackles, tails and streamers of prismatic hues." He doesn't say whether or not the buoyant bodies were made of cork, but that soon became the standard.

Another account states that the cork-bodied bass bug originated in Arkansas and Missouri some time before the turn of the century, where natives made them from beer bottle corks and turkey feathers.

To bring some order out of the multitude of patterns in which bass bugs were being made, some of the early bug makers and bug fishermen got together and decided on a few more or less standard varieties.

Peet's Favorite—White body, brown stripes, white tail and wings.

Dilg's Gem—Orange brown body with black stripes, brown and gray tail, brown turkey wings.

Clarke's Fancy—White body, red tail and wings.

Zane Grey—Gray body, striped tail and wings.

Wilder's Discovery—Body yellow with red stripes, wings yellow and red.

Carter Harrison—Body brown with yellow stripes, fox squirrel wings and tail.

Dr. Henshall—Body tan with red stripes, wings white and red, tail brown.

Dixie Carroll—White body, black stripes, golden pheasant wings and tail.

Hank's Creation—Body silver, wings duck and crimson, tail white.

St. John's Pal—Body red with black stripes, wings mallard, tail yellow.

Chadwick's Sunbeam—Body yellow with black stripes, wings peacock-eyed, tail red.

The early cork-bodied bass bugs were blunt on the front end. B. F. Wilder was apparently the man who first rounded that cork body into a streamlined head, and they became Wilder's Minnows —often called feather minnows. With improvements by Will H. Dilg, a bass bug became popular which was known as the Wilder-Dilg fly, and was made and marketed by Heddon for years.

In the mid-thirties E. H. Peckinpaugh, who was on the scene much earlier with his bass bugs, dished out the face of that cork body and produced the popping bug. Peck's poppers are still being manufactured, and are one of the best known fly-rod bass lures on the market. The Peck bug is made in the feather minnow style as well as the popper.

One of the oldest of the United States manufacturers of flies,

Slim-Bug

Popper-Imp

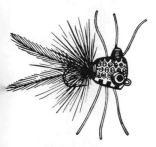

Scaly Popper

Crazy-Pop

Zebra Popper

Creepy Nitwit

Weber's popping bugs are favorite fly-rod lures for bass. Fished on the surface and retrieved in short jerks, they can provide exciting sport.

Whiskerbug

Fly Rod Frog

Fly Rod Mousie

Henshall Lure

Popular Weber fly-rod lures for surface fishing. Whiskerbug is an original design. The Henshall lure, a great topwater killer, is made of deer hair.

including those for bass, is now the Weber Tackle Company, of Stevens Point, Wisconsin. It had its beginning in 1896 when Carrie Frost started tying flies for her father, who was an ardent fisherman. Demand for her products grew and, inevitably, she had to hire helpers to meet it.

In 1920 the business became the Frost Fishing Tackle Company; in 1926, the Weber Lifelike Fly Company; and in 1958, the Weber Tackle Company. Although it now is vastly expanded, offering all types of lures and terminal tackle, the Weber Company still markets a large number of fly-rod bass lures, including the Henshall Lure, a fine topwater bug made of deer hair.

Flies are not as popular as bass bugs and the fly-spinner combination, but they are very effective. Fished dry or wet, some of them are deadly. Two of the most effective are the Woolly Worm and the Muddler Minnow. The Worm, according to Al McClane in his *The Practical Fly Fisherman*, began life in the Missouri Ozarks as a bass fly, before finally going west and becoming best known as a trout fly. Another good one is the Whiskerbug, an original Weber design.

Another noted tackle company which began as a fly-tying venture and expanded to many tackle products is Glen L. Evans, Inc., of Caldwell, Idaho. Mr. Glen L. Evans founded it in 1922, and is still president of the firm. In addition to all types of fly-fishing lures, including a wide variety of bass bugs, this company produces the popular Herb's Dilly and Shyster bass lures.

George I. Phillips founded another business for making flies in 1937 at Alexandria, Pennsylvania, and the Phillips Fly and Tackle Company is today a significant manufacturer of lures. It makes several varieties of bass flies and bugs, and also the very good top-water casting plug called the Crippled Killer.

Bucktails And Jigs

It was only short steps from the ancient fly and the old "bob" to a bucktail or a jig. Only the addition of weight was needed.

Bucktails and jigs both found favor first with saltwater anglers, but then bass fishermen found that they would take fish. Ingenious anglers soon started combining various combinations of bucktails, jigs, spoons and spinners, frequently added a strip or chunk of pork rind, and a whole new series of lures was born. Favorite salt-water spoons such as Weber's Mr. Champ took a trip inland, and have become great bass catchers.

One type of lure which evolved consisted of a weighted hook of some sort preceded by a spinner, with the hook concealed or decorated either with a pork rind strip, a bucktail or a rubber skirt. At their best in shallow water, and essentially weedless, this group is typified by such standards as the Shimmy Wiggler, the Hawaiian Wiggler and the Herb's Dilly.

The Shimmy Wiggler, known as the Al Foss Shimmy Wiggler, came first. It used a bucktail tied hook, and was at its best when armed with a strip of pork rind.

Fred Arbogast patented the rubber skirt, hung it on his various Hawaiian Wigglers, and had an effective exclusive for years. The Hawaiian Wiggler is still a great lure without which no tackle box is complete. Arbogast began his business about 1924, and it will come as a surprise to many to know that his first lure was the Tin Liz, which preceded the Wiggler by some four years.

J. M. Herbert, of Shreveport, Louisiana, a jeweler who is an ardent fisherman, began improving the Shimmy, seeking a lure which would run on the surface even when retrieved slowly. As often happens, he was pushed into making the Herb's Dilly commercially when fishermen of the area saw how effective it was. The Dilly is now produced by the Glen L. Evans Company.

A variation of this spinner-leadhead-bucktail combination came along even earlier, in 1915, when the Shannon Twin Spinner first made the scene. On it the spinners were attached to the ends of short wire which served as weed guards, so that the spinners rode just above the weighted, hook-equipped bucktail. The Shannon

Four favorites from the Fred Arbogast Company (l to r): Hawaiian Wiggler, Hula Popper, Jitterbug, Arbogaster.

Shannon Twin Spinner (left), a safety-pin lure, and two variations of fishing it. Versatile safety-pins can be fished deep or shallow.

Twin Spinner is still a fine bass lure, but it was also the forerunner of another amazingly successful group.

The first of this group was the Helldiver. Made by Howser in St. Louis, with a beginning in the mid-forties, the Helldiver was the first of the "safety pin" lures. It consisted of a spinner on one end of a V-shaped wire, and a weighted hook adorned with a skirt on the other. At the apex of the "V" was a loop, just as you have at one end of a safety pin, and that was the point of attachment for your fishing line. It was an instant success, effective when fished either shallow or deep. The spinner-skirt combination was a killer, and still is.

There are many of these safety-pin lures on the market now, with most sections of the country having their own favorites. Many anglers make their own, actually using safety pins in the process many times. By changing the size and shape and location of the weight on the hook, the size and shape of the spinner, and the size and color of the skirt, this safety pin actually becomes a family of lures. Among the better known are the H & H, Rider, Bushwacker, Busy Body, Machete and Tarantula.

If I could choose only one lure for bass fishing, I'd think long and hard before passing up the safety pin. It is extremely versatile, since it can be fished on top, shallow, deep or bumped off the bottom.

Spoons, Spinners And Plugs

The wobbling spoon had its beginning, according to legend, in 1830, when Julio T. Buel, of Whitehall, New York, was eating his lunch upon the bank of Lake Bomoseen and accidentally dropped his teaspoon into the water. Buel was amazed to see a large fish hit the spoon before it completed its gyrating course to the lake bottom. Buel took an old brass teaspoon, soldered a hook on one end and fashioned the handle into a line-tie.

Buel's spoon proved to be so successful that he began manufacturing metal lures in 1848, and in 1852 took out the first patent in the United States for trolling spoons and spinner baits. Others soon began making metal lures in competition with Buel. Among the earliest was Gardiner M. Skinner, of Clayton, New York, and Skinner spoons and spinners are still on the market today. The Shakespeare Company, better known now for rods and reels, marketed some of the first metal surface or "near surface" lures. Named Revolution and Shakespeare-Worden Bucktail Bait, they were slender aluminum tubes with counter revolving spinners, the latter equipped with a bucktail. Another prominent manufacturer, Pflueger (Enterprise Manufacturing Company), marketed a line of spoons and spinners, and is also credited with being the first to use luminous paint.

Shortly before the turn of the century Jim Heddon was sitting on the bank of Dowagiac Creek, in Michigan, whittling and waiting for a fishing companion. When he tossed the whittled stick into the water to watch it float away, he was startled to see a bass smash into the floating bit of wood.

As any fisherman would have done under the circumstances, Heddon whittled more wooden sticks and hung hooks on them.

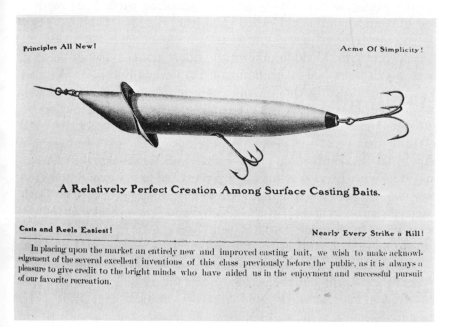

Principles All New!   Acme Of Simplicity!

A Relatively Perfect Creation Among Surface Casting Baits.

Casts and Reels Easiest!   Nearly Every Strike a Kill!

In placing upon the market an entirely new and improved casting bait, we wish to make acknowledgement of the several excellent inventions of this class previously before the public, as it is always a pleasure to give credit to the bright minds who have aided us in the enjoyment and successful pursuit of our favorite recreation.

One of the earliest bass plugs was this lure made by James Heddon in 1898 and advertised in his first catalog. Heddon began making bass plugs in the kitchen of his home in Dowagiac, Michigan, was so successful that he expanded his operation to become one of the leading manufacturers of tackle in the country.

For a few years he whittled and painted the plugs by hand, giving them to friends, and their success with them created such a demand that a new lure company was born. In 1898 Heddon and his two sons, Charles and William, started James Heddon's Sons—in Mrs. Heddon's kitchen. Today the firm is the largest lure manufacturer in the world.

Other materials soon came to join feathers, deer hair, metal and wood in the manufacture of lures. Both Pflueger and Shakespeare made lures from soft rubber, and Pflueger had one made of silk. Then, in 1930, Heddon made the first plastic lure, and a new world was opened for plug makers. Far more lures are now made of plastic than of wood, and production is vastly simplified.

Despite this, some fishermen still prefer the wooden lures, and some companies still make them. Heddon, for instance, abandoned wood completely for a year or two, but then came back with a line of wooden lures and called them the Wooden Classics. They are still available in plastic, but also—at a higher price—in wood.

Along with Heddon, there are other famous names in bass lures. South Bend had its beginning in 1893 when Frank G. Worden began the Worden Bucktail Manufacturing Company in South Bend, Indiana. He changed the name to the South Bend Bait Company in 1910, and continued to produce bucktail flies and wobblers until 1916. In that year Ivar Hennings developed the topwater bass lure which has become synonymous with South Bend—the Bass-Oreno. In 1965 South Bend was bought by the Gladding Corporation, and now has its headquarters in South Otselic, New York. The Bass-Oreno is still a mainstay in the South Bend line and like all of the other plugs in that line is still made of wood. My first bass lure was a Bass-Oreno, and I still have it. It has survived almost three decades.

Creek Chub Bait Company began in 1908 in Garrett, Indiana, where it still turns out thousands of bass killers which are bywords among anglers—Darter, Injured Minnow, Plunker and Pikie. The Injured Minnow is now made only in plastic, but the others are available in either wood or plastic.

The Shannon Twin Spinner was first marketed in 1915, and patented in 1918, by the inventor J. P. Shannon; and this excellent bass lure is still prominent in the line of the Shannon Lure Company of Chicago. It was manufactured by the W. J. Jamison Company under a license granted them by Shannon from the early 1920's until about 1951, at which time control of the company was transferred to J. Max Shannon, son of the inventor. In 1965 he changed the name to Shannon Lure Company, Division of Jamison Tackle Corporation.

Another great lure first reached the market in 1917, after several years of development by the inventor, Lou Eppinger, of Dearborn, Michigan. It was the Dardevle, which is still manufactured in quantity by the Lou J. Eppinger Mfg. Company of Dearborn. Eppinger, who died in 1958, named the lure after the marines who fought in World War I. They were called the Dare Devils by the Allies, but Eppinger misspelled it as "Dardevle" to avoid criticism from those who objected to seeing the word "Devil" in print.

Famous bass spoons (l to r): Dardevle, Sidewinder, Gypsy King, Mr. Champ, Johnson Silver Minnow.

Another spoon which has become a standard was invented in 1920 by Louis Johnson, a retired Chicago foundry operator. He used a single hook soldered firmly to the inside of the bowl, and developed for it a weed guard which went far toward insuring its success. It was the Johnson Silver Minnow, often called the Johnson Spoon. Johnson died in 1933, but the Silver Minnow continues to roll from the Louis Johnson Company plant in Highland Park, Illinois.

Charles Helin developed the first Flatfish in 1933 and has sold more than 32 million of them since then. One of the unusual features of this lure is the offset hooking arrangement. Helin uses a crossbar with a very small treble hook on each end of it. The Helin Tackle Company, in Detroit, Michigan, is still going strong, and is still owned and operated by Charles Helin.

In the mid-thirties several fishermen around Fort Dodge, Iowa, began whittling a wooden lure which became popular, and in the late 1930's brothers Joe and Rudy Kautzky began manufacturing the Lazy Ike. A number of other lures have been added to the line since then, but the Lazy Ike Corporation is still best known for the original plug.

The Garcia Corporation, of Teaneck, New Jersey, has become a giant among tackle manufacturers in less than two decades. In recent years it has placed in the hands of fishermen a staggering amount of rods, reels, lines and lures. The Abu-Reflex is best known, and is an excellent bass lure. The Abu is one of a class of spinner lures which are popular and effective. It has a slender, weighted body preceded by a spinner, trailed by a treble hook tied with a combination of hackle and feathers.

The Mepps French spinners, imported by Sheldons', Inc., of Antigo, Wisconsin, is a similar lure which has been amazingly effective. It is available in sizes from 1/12 ounce to one ounce, with or without bucktails.

Types Of Bass Plugs

Plugs, as contrasted with spoons, spinners and jigs, evolved into four types: 1) topwater lures; 2) sinking lures; 3) surface lures which are shallow runners on the retrieve; and 4) surface lures which run deep when retrieved.

The first Heddon lure fell into the first class, the pure topwater; and a 1966 Heddon offering in the same category is the Chugger. Heddon's first catalog, issued in 1902, listed only the Dowagiac top-water lure, but the next one in 1903 also offered the first sinking plug. It was called the Dowagiac Underwater, and a weight attached to a screw eye on the bottom of the lure kept it from floating. Classic example of a modern Heddon sinking lure is the River Runt.

In the 1910 catalog Heddon listed the first example of a lure in the third class, a floater which was a shallow runner on the retrieve. It was called the Dowagiac Swimming Minnow, and was dropped from the catalog in 1914, but reappeared in a different form in 1917 as the 1600 and 1700 series. The modern counterpart is the Lucky 13, although its appearance is entirely different.

That same 1917 catalog revealed a new lure called the Crab Wiggler, which was the forerunner of one of the most successful types of lures on the market today. It was pointed at both ends, floated when at rest, was retrieved backwards, and dove on the retrieve because of a metal collar. It was a highly successful lure in the Heddon line for years.

Four basic types of bass plugs (l to r): Chuggar, a floater; River Runt, a sinker; Lucky 13, floating-diving; Bomber, floats at rest and runs deep on the retrieve.

Famous floaters-shallow runners (l to r): Babe Oreno, Lucky 13, Darter, Floating River Runt, Jointed Vamp.

Famous floaters-deep divers (l to r): Hellbender, Lazy Ike, Flatfish, Big Dig, Bomber.

Famous surface lures (l to r): Tiny Torpedo, Crippled Killer, Zaragossa, Zara Spook, Devils Horse, Chugger, Paw Paw, Devils Warhorse, Dalton Special, Darter, Chunker, Skip-Jack, Skip-N-Cisco.

Present-day examples of lures in the fourth class are the Bomber and Whopper-Stopper, and their stable-mates, the Water Dog and the Hellbender. The first Bomber was made in 1942, and a patent granted for it in 1948.

The Vibrating Lure

Except for those who have read my articles in newspapers and magazines, many anglers have probably never heard of Bill Adcock, but this Baton Rouge fisherman has had a pronounced effect on bass fishing in all parts of the nation.

For years after the first wooden plugs appeared, and after Heddon introduced the first plastic baits in 1930, underwater lures had two actions only. They either wobbled and darted, or they came straight through the water with no action at all except that produced by spinners fore and aft, or by the angler's manipulation.

Adcock developed the notched River Runt, a lure that vibrates on the retrieve. The mechanics of "notching" are simple. First, he clipped the loose ring from the screw eye and threw it away. Next, he filed a smooth notch on the top side of that screw eye. Last, he tied the monofilament leader to the screw eye with a figure 8 knot, pulling the knot down into the notch tightly.

The most important effect of this alteration was that it held the front end of the lure fast, keeping it from wobbling. As speed of retrieve was increased the rear of the lure began to quiver and vibrate. Tying the leader on top of the screw eye had the added advantage of tilting the lure downward, making it run a bit deeper. Sticking the rod full length down into the water while making the retrieve got still more depth.

In Louisiana in the late forties it was common for a fisherman using a notched Runt to catch ten or twenty times as many bass as another using the factory version. It was that much more effective, and it still is.

Along came a lure from the Texas coast, where it was used for saltwater fishing, and somebody discovered it would vibrate without notching if the back hooks were removed. It was called the Fisherman's Favorite, and we began alternating it with the notched Runt.

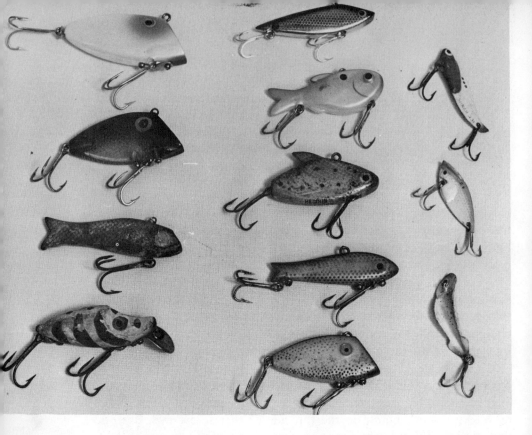

Vibrating lures: (left row, from top) Bayou Boogie, Pico Perch, Fisherman's Favorite, Notched River Runt; (middle row) Hot Spot, Tru-Shad, Super Sonic, Mitey Minnow, Swimmin' Minnow; (right row) Sonar, Gay Blade, Spoonplug.

Then came the factory-made vibrating lures. First was the Pico Perch, made by the Padre Island Company at Corpus Christi. Later came the Bayou Boogie, begun in Monroe, Louisiana; and the Swimmin Minnow, in Shreveport, Louisiana. And then Heddon's Sonic; and the Tru-shad, Gay Blade and Hot Spot.

The notched Midget River Runt is still very effective, and some anglers still use it extensively, but the built-in quiver of factory-made lures has virtually eliminated the necessity for this bit of angler ingenuity.

With his notching method of fishing Bill Adcock brought one other dimension to bass fishing—speed of retrieve. Until that time "the slower the better" had been the rule for retrieves, but that quickly was discarded. We ran the notched Runts as fast as we could crank the reel handle, and we learned that there is no such

Bill Adcock, who developed the notched River Runt, holds hefty proof of its effectiveness as a bass lure. The Runt, shown in close-up at right, was turned into a vibrating lure by removing the ring from the screw-eye, then filing a notch on top of the screw-eye so the leader would not slip.

thing as pulling a lure too fast for a bass to catch it if he wants it. I am fully convinced that the speed of the lure itself is often sufficient to trigger the strike of a bass. There are times and there are places, let me emphasize, when a wobbling type of lure fished very slowly will take more bass than will a vibrating plug fished fast. Inflexible rules have no place in bass fishing.

The Spoonplug

Designed by Buck Perry, the Spoonplug is a metal, sinking lure, and is made in a number of sizes. The smaller ones are for working shallow water, and the bigger the lure the deeper it will run on a normal retrieve.

As with the notched River Runt, the smaller Spoonplugs will vibrate on a fast retrieve, and will stay in the water at very high speed. Perry designed them for working the shallows when bass have moved in close to shore.

His bigger Spoonplugs are designed for fishing *on* the bottom of the lake, for "walking" the bottom, as Perry puts it.

The "Stick"

Fishermen are prone to do all manner of strange things to bass plugs in an effort to make the factory brand better, and occasionally one of the derivations results in a new lure. So it was with the "stick."

This version originated on one of the lakes of northwest Louisiana, probably Black Lake, when fishermen removed the spinners from the topwater Paw Paw and added a small weight where the rear spinner had been. That simple move changed the lure completely. The plug that resulted did resemble a "stick."

The weight added at the rear of the Paw Paw, usually a sparkplug nut, was just enough to pull that end under water slightly. The result was that the lure floated, but at an angle, with the nose sticking out of the water a bit. The only action the plug has is that imparted by the angler. It bounces and darts when worked in short, crisp pulls, but disturbs the water little since the nose is rounded or pointed. It catches bass in numbers.

Jack Smithwick, of Shreveport, Louisiana, made the first com-

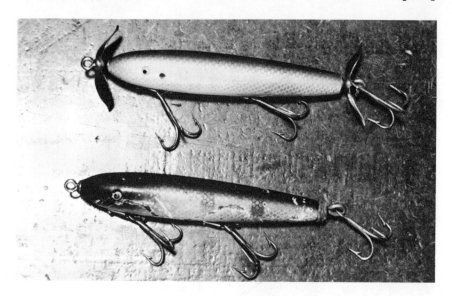

Paw Paw bass plug (top) becomes a "stick" lure when spinners are removed and a weight added at the rear. Lure floats with the nose sticking out of the water; when given the proper action it's deadly.

mercial version of the "stick." He called it the Devils Warhorse, and it is still available in a number of sizes and versions.

Smithwick's Devils Horse has been more successful nation-wide than has the Warhorse. It has spinners, floats on the surface in a horizontal position, and makes the fuss that spinners usually do. It is an excellent lure, as are such other spinner-type topwaters as the Paw Paw, the Injured Minnow, the Nip-I-Diddee and the Crippled Killer.

Heddon came out with a "stick" called the Dying Quivver, made of plastic (Smithwick's is still made of wood), but it was dropped from the catalog after a few years. I suspect that angler resistance to the "no-action" topwater was the cause.

The Bomber Bait Company, of Gainesville, Texas, added a "stick" to its line and called it the Bomber Stick, and it is still marketed.

Heddon has two lures in the line which are spinnerless top-water and which are pointed or rounded at the ends, but neither

Rapala lures, first made of balsa wood, now of buoyant plastic, have earned a nationwide reputation as bass-killing surface plugs.

duplicates the action of a "stick." They're the Zaragossa and the Zara Spook. The Zaragossa has been in the line for almost half a century, and the Zara Spook for more than a quarter of a century. Florida has been the stronghold of the Zara, but this big, bait-casting lure is now becoming popular in many other parts of the nation.

The Rapala Lures

Less than a decade ago an extremely buoyant surface lure made of balsa wood made its appearance on the market. It was the Rapala. Difficult to cast because of its lightness and wind resistance, this minnow-like lure was an instant success because it caught fish.

The demand for Rapalas far exceeded the supply and, as always is true in such a situation, American manufacturers came to the rescue. Now in the field with their own versions of this type of lure—most of them made of buoyant plastic—are Plastics Research and

Development Corporation, with the Rebel; Heddon, with the Cobra; Whopper Stopper, with the Hellcat; Smithwick with the Rogue; Bagley with the Bang O Lure; and Cordell with the Red Fin.

The Jitterbug

A unique topwater lure which deserves special mention is the Jitterbug, made by the Fred Arbogast Company. It has a built-in action on a steady retrieve, with a "plop-plop-plop" sound that is often deadly to bass, and it has been a popular lure in all parts of the nation since it was introduced about 1937. Heddon's Crazy Crawler is a lure which has similar action, and both are particularly effective at night.

Favorites—Mine and Yours

Let's canvass the country and look at the favorite bass lures in different sections, as recommended by some of the best fishermen in those areas.

The Northwest—Ed Fredrich, of Seattle: Rebel, Creek Chub Injured Minnow, Whopper Stopper, Bomber, Hustler, Rex Weedless Spoon.

Northeast—Dick Jennings, of Cortland, New York: Dardevle, Hula Popper, Flatfish, Jitterbug and Rebel.

North Central—Stu Mann, of Detroit Lakes, Minnesota, and Ray Gray, of Chicago: Walkie-Talkie, The Amazin Maizie, Hula Popper, Johnson Silver Minnow with pork chunk, Cisco Kid and fly-rod popping bugs.

The West—Joe Mears, of Altadena, California: Bomber, Hellbender, Sonic, Hotshot, Bass-Oreno, Lazy Ike, River Runt, Dardevle, plastic worms.

Midwest—Pete Czura, of Lincoln, Nebraska: Hula Popper, Sonic, black eels, plastic worms, Mepps Spinners.

New England—Bob Elliot, of Augusta, Maine: Jitterbug, spoons, fly rod popping bugs, imitation frogs, streamer and bucktail flies such as the Mickey Finn, dry flies such as the large Wulff patterns, small spinners, weighted jig with a hair skirt.

To forty-six of the best bass fishermen I know, scattered throughout the nation, I put two questions: 1. What is your favorite

Collecting lures, one of the side pleasures of bass fishing, grew into a hobby for Clyde Harbin of Memphis, shown here with part of his collection of old-timers.

bass lure? 2. Which lure would you choose if you could have only one with which to do all your bass fishing?

Here are their answers: Shimmy Wiggler, plastic worm, jig and eel, Hellbender, Lucky 13, Zara Spook, Johnson Silver Minnow with plastic worm, Chugger, Doll Fly, Rebel, Bass Buster marabou jig, River Runt, Hula Popper, Hawaiian Wiggler, Jitterbug, spoon, Devils Horse, safety pin lure, Pico Perch, Dardevle, Sonar, popping bug, Devils Warhorse, Bayou Boogie, jigs and Rapala-type lures.

Many of the same lures cropped up time and again, with these being repeated many times: safety-pin lures, plastic worms, jig and eel, Johnson Silver Minnow and jigs.

Another question put to these experts was: "How much did your biggest bass weigh, and what did you catch him on?"

Those lunkers ranged up to a heady 16 3/4 pounds, and here are some of the lures they were taken on: safety-pin lure, plastic worm, Hellbender, jig and eel, Zara Spook, Shimmy Wiggler, Hell-diver, Hawaiian Wiggler, Chugger, Dalton Special, "stick," Pikie Minnow, Crippled Killer, Mr. Champ, Bomber, Fidgit, Shannon Spinner, Devils Horse, Rapala and Red Fin.

There are many excellent lures which never get national distribution, or which never become popular nationwide, but which enjoy tremendous popularity in a state or a region. Other fine ones enjoy a period of prosperity, either locally or nationally, then fade from the picture.

I believe that bass strike because they are either hungry, angry or curious. My search for lures which will elicit one of these reactions just a bit better, or more often, insures that my tackle box will always runneth over.

CHAPTER FOURTEEN

The Plastic Worm

THE first plastic worm to become popular was what is known as a "rigged worm." The worm was attached to a length of monofilament nylon having two or three hooks plus a spinner of sorts and perhaps a red bead or two out front. It was deadly and still is, particularly when bass are in the shallows. These rigged worms were then the only kind on the market. But some anglers soon began rearranging the imitation crawlers in several ways. One of the first and most effective changes was to remove the worm from the rig and simply use it on a single hook. By sticking the point of the hook into the body of the worm they made it "weedless." Fishermen had been killing big bass on pork eels for some time, fishing them on the bottom, so it was a short step to weighting one of the weedless worms and crawling it along the bottom in the same fashion. It is a deadly lure.

Just why the plastic worm is such an effective lure is still somewhat of a mystery, but you can catch more bass on plastic worms than you can on nightcrawlers or earthworms. Perhaps it's because the plastic ones are tougher and can be cast without coming apart, and can be chewed on without breaking to pieces. The important thing is that the artificials work, are easier to get than real worms, last longer, are cleaner to use and probably cost less in the long run.

Bass feed on small eels and on snakes at times, but not to the extent that would suggest the phenomenal success of plastic worms. Undoubtedly, one of the main reasons for their effectiveness, in addition to their lifelike appearance, is that plastic worms *feel* lifelike to a bass. The fish does not readily eject the lure if he's not immediately hooked, as he almost invariably does with a hard lure. Bass will, in fact, pick up a plastic worm and swallow it completely.

The ingenuity of bass anglers and manufacturers knows no bounds, so it is not surprising that a worm lure appeared which, when cast and retrieved, came back with a swimming motion. One of the first was the El Tango. Other manufacturers soon followed suit, and most have such offerings now. Burke came up with their Jig-A-Do head to accomplish the same thing in a different manner.

Bass fishermen have experimented with plastic worms in a multitude of ways, and most of their creations have caught fish. They have fished them with almost every conceivable type of

First plastic worms, which appeared in the mid-fifties, were rigged with three hooks snelled together and a spinner and beads in front.

spinner, hook and leadhead, and have garnished most other lures by hanging a worm on them.

Colored Worms

Every earthworm I have ever seen was red, brown or some shade in between, and the first plastic worms to create interest were red. Soon came black, and those two colors were standard for quite a while. Today, the catalog sheet for one worm manufacturer shows fifty-two different colors and color combinations. In addition to such mild numbers as dark blue, light blue, purple, green and yellow, there are more exotic offerings such as yellow with black spots, modulated dark blue and white, black glitter and red with white head. All of these worms catch bass. I have never seen a purple worm, but this color is currently the big bass killer of the worm set.

The important point is that color *does* make a difference in plastic worms. It is irrelevant whether it is something about the purple dye that makes the worm attract more bass bites than does some other color. There are times when purple worms will take many more bass than will blue worms fished from the same boat in the same spot—or vice versa. This being the case, any angler who doesn't experiment with various colors is missing a bet. You don't have to get *all* the colors available, but make sure you have purple, blue, black and red.

Harnessed Worms

Depending upon how much hardware there is on it, a harnessed worm sinks slowly to moderately fast. You can catch bass on one by simply casting it into the shallows and reeling it back slowly.

You can increase the action, which may or may not bring more strikes, by twitching the worm along on your retrieve in little jerks alternated with pauses. Try little twitches and big, sudden ones and slow ones. Experiment until you find which technique gets results.

To keep the worm shallow, keep your rod tip high and/or increase the speed of retrieve. To fish deeper, simply let the worm sink before you begin your retrieve. If you are casting against a bank where it is impractical to let the worm sink, begin your re-

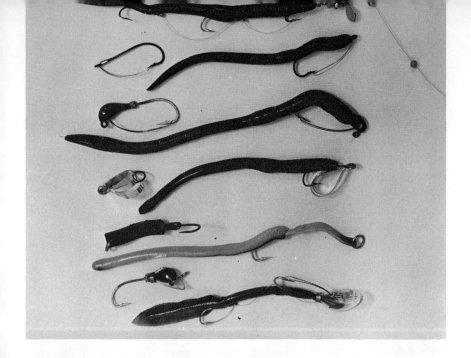

Anglers have devised various methods of rigging plastic worms (from top): harnessed worm with spinner and beads; worm on a weedless hook; worm on Cordell's Banana Head jig; worm on a Sneeky Neeky weedless hook; El Tango rig; Jig-a-Doo rig.

Bottom-bumping weedless leadhead worm rigs (from top): leadhead without weed guard, hook buried in worm; leadhead with weed guard; bucktail jig with weed guard.

Worm on a weedless leadhead jig (left) and a worm-rigged Doll Fly on the bottom of a tank of water show how the lures behave on lake bottom.

trieve immediately but then begin your pauses to let it sink about every 5 or 10 feet.

Harnessed worms are available with weedless hooks, and if there is a danger of getting hung up where you fish, you should use these. I find little if any difference in the hooking efficiency of good weedless hooks and those without weed guards. When you feel a bass take your harnessed worm, strike immediately. The odds are good that one of the two or three hooks will take hold. If you wait, the bass may decide that two or three hooks and a spinner don't add much to the taste of a worm.

Single-Hook Worms

Most worms will sink slowly, even if they're "floaters," with the added weight of one bass-sized hook, and for most fishing in relatively shallow lakes this is perfect. Fish the single-hook worm just as you would the harnessed worm, except that, since it has no spinner, you must provide all the action by manipulating your rod and reel.

The big difference here is that you should not strike immediately when you feel a bass take the worm. With just that single hook in the head, it is probable that the bass doesn't have the lure entirely in his mouth and thus would not be hooked.

When retrieving the single-hook worm, you must be alert to feel the slightest resistance, for frequently a bass will mouth the bait gingerly. When this happens you have two courses of action: 1. Give him all the slack he wants. 2. Keep a slight resistance on the line but stop reeling; let the bass pull your rod down to the surface of the water, then hit him.

Bass will vary tremendously in how they take a worm from day to day and week to week. I try to start my worming by giving the fish little time, then gradually increase it if need be to start hooking them. The longer you wait the better the odds that the bass will wrap your line around a stump—but it may be necessary to chance that in order to hook the fish.

The single-hook worm is more versatile than the harnessed worm because you can fish it right on the bottom, in shallow or in deep water. Unless the bottom is unusually clean, this calls for some kind of weedless hook. I use a weedless hook much of the time, but frequently I make a plain hook weedless by burying the point in the body of the worm. This latter method even seems to be more effective at times, possibly because there is less hardware showing.

Keep in mind at all times when fishing plastic worms that the less weight you use the better, for that means less resistance for the fish to feel when he picks the lure up. To fish the worm deep, however, you must compromise on this rule and add some kind of weight to get it down.

As mentioned previously, the bare hook will slowly sink most worms, even the floating kind. With any wind or current, however, add a split shot on the line 4 to 6 inches from the hook. No. 7 is the best size to begin with; if that's not enough, either add a second one or change to a bigger size. When you are fishing in water that is at least 8 to 10 feet deep, using a weight with the worm saves a great deal of time waiting for the lure to reach the bottom, and more than compensates for the few fish lost which feel the resistance of the weight.

Other lures are often garnished with plastic worms (from top): Hawaiian Wiggler, Upperman Bucktail, Doll Fly, Johnson Silver Minnow.

Four of the many ways to fish the single-hook plastic worm (from top): single hook with point buried in the worm to make it weedless, no sinker; weedless hook used with a pear-shaped sinker which slides free on line to allow bass to run with worm without feeling drag; weedless hook with barrel sinker which slides free on line; weedless hook with split shot on line.

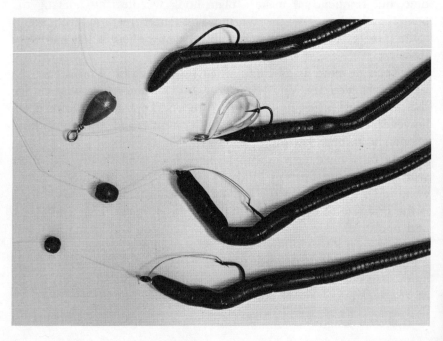

Another method of adding weight is to use a sinker which allows the line to run freely through it when a bass picks up the worm. I prefer the barrel sinker with a hole through the middle, but others like the pear-shaped sinker with a wire loop at the top.

The leadhead jig, such as Cordell's Banana Jig, is simply a weighted worm with the weight integral with the hook. The weed guard and its banana shape enable it to slip over limbs and rocks and through weeds without snagging. It's a combination which can be fished under the most adverse conditions.

Here again, use the lightest jig necessary to get your worm down in a reasonable length of time. If you're working water that's 30 or 40 feet deep, for instance, a 3/8-ounce jig is usually preferable to a 1/4-ounce head. It just saves a lot of time waiting for the lure to reach bottom.

At times bass will take a plastic worm attached to a weighted bucktail such as the Upperman when they won't take either of the two alone. Arming a marabou or polar-bear hair jig such as the Doll Fly or Bass Buster with a worm will trigger a strike on other occasions.

Know The Action

Regardless of which type of hookup you use, to handle it effectively you must know exactly how it performs under all conditions. You can learn that by practicing with it in clear, shallow water where you can actually watch the action. Watch the attitude the worm assumes when lying motionless on the bottom. It will vary greatly depending upon what rig you're using and what worm you're using. Memorize the action it takes when you manipulate rod and reel in various ways. Crawl it slowly over the bottom; twitch it up and let it settle again repeatedly; sweep your rod tip high, then take up line slack as you let the worm sink back to the bottom; reel in the worm with an undulating motion, never quite letting it hit the bottom. If you haven't done this, you will be surprised at what you see. You will suddenly realize just how important it is to know what action you're giving that worm down below.

Find a treetop where you can experiment and see what you're

doing. Let that worm sink down through the branches, retrieve it in a variety of ways and see exactly what happens. Learn to feel a limb as you reel the worm up against it, let off 2 or 3 inches of slack, bounce the worm gently over that limb, and immediately let it drop back down.

When To Strike

Worming is a game of *feel*. Develop your sense of touch. Hold your rod lightly when making a retrieve, but be in full control of it so that you detect the slightest pull on the worm. If you feel resistance and aren't sure whether it's bass or bottom or limb, hold that exact position without moving the rod and without reeling for a few seconds. If it is a bass you'll be able to tell it and give him line.

Setting the hook on a bass after you've given him line requires quite a bit of doing. Many times the fish will move obliquely away from or toward you, so that there will be a bow in the line. Best bet is to get your rod tip down near the water, reaching as far out toward the fish as possible and then, when you have guessed that the bass has had time enough to get the hook in his mouth, sweep the rod back vigorously but smoothly. This doesn't look nearly as classy and professional as a quick flick of the rod tip, but the latter will get you more grief than bass when you're fishing a worm.

It is obvious that, in order to let a bass have line, you must disengage whatever type of retrieving apparatus you're using. If it is a spincasting reel, you just push the button; a spinning reel, flip the bail or pickup open; freespool casting reel, push the button. A conventional casting reel without free spooling is not nearly as suitable for this type of fishing as are the first three, since it is difficult to give line without having the bass feel the resistance. It can be done, however, by manually feeding line off the spool.

It frequently happens that a bass will stay in the same spot after picking up the worm. Most of the time you still must wait before setting the hook while the bass "gloms" the worm.

Sam Welch, of Bull Shoals, Arkansas, one of the very best of the worm fishermen, explains the above term as follows: "For the benefit of the uninitiated 'glom' is a local derivation of the word 'glomeration,' meaning that bass chew on a plastic worm like a cow on her cud until, eventually, they ball it up inside the mouth. Granting the assumption is correct, it is little wonder that it is difficult to set a hook hard enough to penetrate the coiled layers of the plastic product and still make contact."

That brings up another point. When you make a hook weedless by burying the point in the worm, remember that you must strike unusually hard to get that hook back out and into the bass.

When fishing a worm tie your monofilament line or leader directly to the lure. Do not use a snap or a snap swivel, for either will adversely affect the efficiency of the worm.

Worms On Top

Learn to work a single-hook worm across the surface of the water, never letting it get more than 6 inches deep. By quickly and continuously twitching your rod tip and reeling in jerks you can cause the worm to undulate across the surface just as a snake swims. When you can handle it this way, take it to a topwater situation and watch out. Bass hit this bait with a vengeance. Be prepared to give complete slack at the strike, wait, then set the hook.

Most of the floating worms will actually float with a hook *if* the hook is small and light. Some of the newer super-floatables will float with just about any single hook in them. These have one particular application in addition to those you'll probably dream up. Ease your boat along in the shallows during the spawning season and watch for a bass chasing intruders from his (or her) nest. When you find one get in position to cast, wait for the bass to rush away again, then quickly drop the worm over the nest while papa or mama is away. A bass can't stand to come home and find that plastic worm floating over his nest and will hit it hard. A couple of seconds of waiting is usually all that's needed before setting the hook.

Trolling

Trolling a plastic worm can be very effective, although very few fishermen think of working them in this manner. Watch your line carefully to see that it doesn't twist, which it will often do unless you troll very slowly—and sometimes even then. Drifting through a "worm hole" with your plastics bumping the bottom is often deadly.

Worm Holes

These are simply spots in a lake where bass gather in bunches on the bottom, and they have come to be known as worm holes because plastic worms will take fish from them with regularity through the hottest parts of the summer. Standard procedure for many bass anglers, once the dog days set in, is to spend the entire fishing trip making the rounds of their holes.

On Black Lake, just a few miles from my Natchitoches, Louisiana, home, many of these worm holes coincide with the schooling spots where bass break on top after shad. Strangely enough, however, there are some good worm holes where topwater schooling activity is never seen.

As a general rule, plastic worms fished on the bottom become more and more effective as the weather gets hotter and hotter. In cold weather, in these same worm holes, a bucktail such as an Upperman is much more effective than a worm.

Cast-Retrieve-Strike-Fight-Net

Wɪᴛʜ these five topics we come to the core of catching a bass. All else is prelude, but now we are approaching the mechanics of reducing a free fish to possession. Let's look at them in order.

The Cast

Here we are not concerned with the techniques of casting, but rather with the application of the skills you are assumed to have or that you will learn about in later chapters.

Plan your cast to drop the lure *beyond* the spot where you think the bass should be. This is the cardinal rule and should be followed in all instances except where special circumstances dictate otherwise. The object, of course, is to get the lure into the water without frightening the bass, and to work it back *past* the fish.

Elementary? Perhaps, but thousands of bass owe their continued freedom to the fact that this procedure is frequently ignored by fishermen who should know better. Most of them do know better, but they just quit thinking and cast by rote.

Figuratively hitting a bass on the head with the lure is most damaging in the shallows, for that is where they frighten most easily. If the fish are deep, this isn't particularly important.

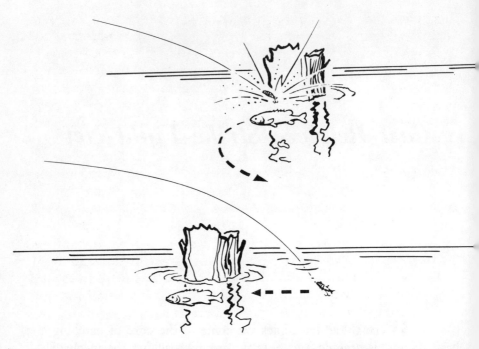

When casting to a likely bass lair in the shallows, don't drop the lure right on the spot you expect a bass to be (top). The splash of the lure will frighten the fish. Cast beyond the lair (bottom) and retrieve the lure past it.

If they are deep, bass aren't likely to be frightened by your lure hitting the water. However, the lure should land far enough beyond the bass's lair so that it will attain the depth at which the fish is lying by the time it passes the spot.

If you are using a floating-diving plug, a certain distance is required before it reaches its running depth regardless of how fast you retrieve. As an example, let's suppose the bass is 12 feet down and that it takes a 10-yard run for your lure to reach that depth. If you drop it only 5 yards beyond the garden spot, it will inevitably pass far above the fish. Even when using a sinking bottom-bumper such as a leadhead worm or a bucktail, there are times when it is more effective to sink it beyond the fish and work it back through.

Impatience causes many fishermen to spoil good spots by casting before they are in proper position. The grass seems to look just a little greener a cast-and-a-half away. Resist the temptation and wait until you're within suitable range before probing that situation.

I mentioned special occasions where dropping the lure *on* the fish, or on the likely lair, is best. This is frequently true with light-weight fly-rod lures, and particularly with topwater ones. It is sometimes true of small, light spinning lures, and rarely with bigger, heavier casting plugs. When bass are slashing into a school of bait fish on the surface; fire that plug right into the middle of the melee.

The trend of late has been to discount the importance of the long cast. You don't have to be a distance-casting champ, but if you can't toss more than three or four boat lengths you need some backyard sessions.

The key is in knowing when to stick with short to medium casts—which will be most of the time—and when to resort to long-range tactics. When you are anchored near a schooling spot, you will catch more bass if you can keep your boat a substantial distance away from the concentration of fish. Thus, the longer casts you can *accurately* make, the better off you are.

A cast can be soft or harsh. You can fire that lure into the water and make a lot of noise, or you can snub your cast down until the lure enters the water almost gently. Which is best? Most of the time the gentle approach, but try the other from time to time. I have found occasions when a big topwater lure splashed into the water attracted strikes rather than frightening the fish.

The Retrieve

Except with surface lures, and those you allow to sink before beginning a retrieve, begin the retrieve even before the lure hits the water. Follow this procedure: Near the end of the cast, snub the lure down gently until it has about lost its forward momentum and begins its fall to the water. By this time have your rod tip pointed toward the lure, almost parallel with the water. End the forward progress of the lure by either thumbing the spool, feathering the line or pushing the button, according to the type of reel you are using. Start it back toward you by raising your rod tip from almost horizontal to almost vertical. Remember that you are doing all this *before* the plug hits the water. While you are sweeping your rod upward begin cranking that reel handle. Thus, when the lure enters the water it is already heading back toward you.

This maneuver is most easily and smoothly accomplished with a conventional, revolving-spool casting reel simply because no other braking system is as efficient and delicate as an educated thumb applied to the spool. It can be done adequately, however, with spinning or spincasting gear.

If you cast right-handed and shift the rod to the left hand for the retrieve, as most do for bait or spincasting, you can make the "rod sweep" maneuver before, during or after you change hands. If you cast with one hand and crank the reel handle with the other, the operation is simplified even further.

This technique of retrieving is valuable for two reasons. First, it starts the lure back toward you in the direction it was designed to move. The plug doesn't splash into the water backwards and *then* reverse directions. By entering the water head first and *continuing* to "swim" in that direction it presents a more natural appearance. Also, the lure disturbs the water less when it enters the water properly and is less likely to frighten the bass, particularly in shallow water, than one which smacks down in an ungainly fashion.

The second reason is that you will hang up less and therefore get more productive retrieves. Many lures are quite "weedless" or "snagless" even when they don't have weed guards as such, but *only* when moving in the direction in which they're designed to move.

In addition to taking full advantage of the inherent weedless properties of some lures, this technique has the added advantage of permitting you to fish a sinking-type lure without letting it sink. Often I have found weed beds loaded with bass which had not more than 6 inches of clear water over them. If the lure sank at all, odds were good it would be fouled with weeds and that cast lost. You can use a topwater lure in such cases, true, but frequently a spinner-skirt affair buzzing overhead triggers many more strikes.

During the retrieve hold your rod handle the way it feels best to you. There isn't much variation in grips with fly or spinning rods, but with spincasting and bait-casting rods you have the alternatives of holding them by the grip, by palming the reel, or in front of the reel.

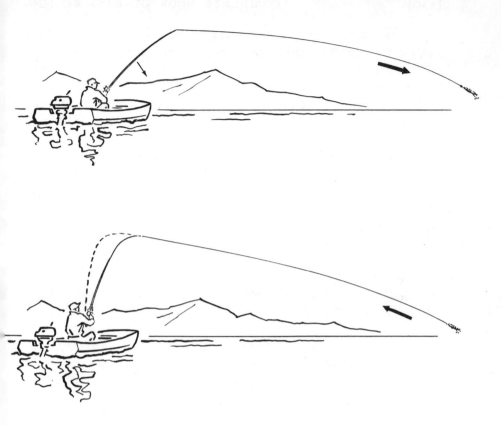

Proper way to begin retrieve is *before* lure hits the water. As the lure nears the target (top), and the rod is approaching the horizontal, snub the reel and halt the forward progress of the lure. Then raise the rod tip (bottom), pulling the lure toward you before it hits the water, and begin reeling at the same time.

The forward grip puts less strain on the wrist muscles, but I don't feel as if I have as much reel control when I'm using it. It became popular in the early days of casting because it was a necessity. There were no level winds, so the angler had to hold the rod this way and manually level-wind the line with his fingers.

Never retrieve with the rod at more than a 90-degree angle to your line, simply because you have nowhere to go with the strike. Conversely, the more room you're likely to need to set the hook, such as when you have slack or bow in the line for any reason, the farther toward the lure you should point your rod.

When executing the maneuver which starts the lure back toward you before it enters the water, you will frequently find that your rod is pointing straight up or even a bit behind you as you sweep it up to reverse the direction of the lure. Get it back down in proper retrieving position as quickly as you can, by reeling rapidly and lowering the rod gradually, seeking to maintain a smooth movement of the lure at all times.

The manner in which you retrieve the lure is the most important mechanical aspect of bass fishing. The weight of your stringer is apt to vary directly with the imagination you display in manipulating the lure during the retrieve. This is true, without exception, for all types of bass lures.

The speed of the retrieve can be slow, medium or fast, but it does not have to be constant. Experiment with many kinds of retrieves. Try retrieves that are slow and ultra-fast, steady and erratic. By using a combination of rod manipulations and reeling maneuvers, you can impart a wide variety of actions to any lure.

Among anglers everywhere, the fast retrieve is one of the most productive with the vibrating-type lures. When a fast, steady retrieve isn't producing, however, try giving that rod handle a quick jerk about every 5 or 10 feet of the retrieve. Now and then it's pure poison. It is possible that a bass sees this erratically retrieved lure as a choice morsel which has an ailment of some sort. It suddenly breaks stride, regains its flight, then falters again. An analogy would be a lion watching a herd of impalas fleeing past the spot where he's crouching. One of the impalas stumbles, falters and falls behind the herd—and the lion attacks.

Just as we learn to manipulate a plastic worm by actually watching the action in clear, shallow water, so can we do the same with other underwater lures. With topwater lures, of course, it is easy to see what action your manipulation is causing.

You will probably find that some of your fishing partners will be able to get more out of a particular lure than you can. They can fish it more effectively, and the reason is that they are imparting a different action to the lure.

The Strike

Now we come to the technique of setting the hook—striking

back when the bass hits. Do it with gusto, with enthusiasm! If you're using a sensible test line and a rod at least 5 or 6 feet long, you can put a lot of muscle into the strike without breaking the line. You must do so, in fact, to get much hook penetration in a bass. The mouth and jaws of a bass are tough, and except at the very corners aren't inclined to tear out readily.

Keeping your hooks very sharp eases the effort needed to sink them past the barbs, but I confess I rely more on a hefty strike than on a honing stone or file. The deeper you are fishing, particularly with slow-moving lures such as plastic worms, the more difficult it is to set the hook and the more important it is to keep your hooks sharp.

When retrieving an underwater lure fairly rapidly, a quick jerk is usually sufficient to hook the bass when you feel him hit. Many times the fish will hook himself, particularly on a rapidly retrieved plug.

In topwater fishing be alert to strike *immediately* when the bass hits. Your reaction time here is slower than with underwater lures, since you must see the bass hit, your eyes must transmit that message to the brain, and the brain must tell the muscles to act. With underwater lures you *feel* the bass hit and your strike is virtually reflex action.

When you feel that you have the bass hooked, don't try to set the hook again and again during the fight that follows. Once the hook is in past the barb, further jerks and heaves on your part can open a sizeable hole around the hook which makes it easier for the fish to unhook himself, particularly when he jumps.

The Fight

Bass do not make long runs when hooked. To free themselves they rely on head shaking, bulldog-like surges and jerks, aerial acrobatics, and on trying to foul line and lure on any obstruction which is convenient. The type of battle you wage depends largely upon which of these tactics the fish is using at the time.

The sense of feel is most important in determining how you play a bass. Specifically, it tells you how much pressure to put on the fish to bring him in, and this comes only with experience. Ideally, you should keep the line tight and the bass coming toward you except when you feel that he is resisting too strongly. Then you should either hold steady or give line. If your reel has a slip clutch, a drag, this removes some of the possibility of angler error in knowing when to "horse him" and when to give him line. If the drag is set properly, it will usually compensate for many human mistakes.

A disadvantage of the drag-equipped reel is that you may need to stop a bass to keep him from getting into a brush pile or around a stump. You can tighten the drag until it won't slip, but then you lose the advantages of the clutch. In a situation like this it's best to manually slow or stop the rush by pressing your finger against the spool of a spinning reel, or your thumb against the spool of a casting reel. Some spincast reels have positive retrieve (no slip clutch action) when the handle is in a forward position, with the drag being operative when the handle is backed off or released. With others, to stop a fish taking line you must push the button and hold it down.

In all of these operations to slow or stop the flight of a bass toward cover, when you render the slip clutch inoperative you should manipulate the rod. Play the fish with the rod at right angles to the line most of the time. By extending your arms, and by pointing the rod more in the direction of the fish, you can effectively give line even though none is leaving the spool. This will often cope with the heavy surges of big bass, which are usually of short duration, but remember to reassume the normal rod position (90-degree angle to the line) as quickly as the fish permits so that you will be ready to repeat the maneuver if need be.

Be especially sensitive to the lunges of a heavy bass when it is near the boat, for this is when most big fish are lost. Here is where your ability to give several feet of line quickly, by manipulating arms and rod, is tremendously important. When you get the bass to the boat, if you're not ready to boat him, leave him 2 or 3 feet from the end of your rod and keep leading him around in figure-eights until you are ready to land him. Anglers lose many bass by failing to do this, for if the angler gets the bass to the boat and then stops, slack will form in his line.

What do you do when a bass jumps? *After* he jumps it is too late to do anything except try to maintain a tight line. Most of the time you will have warning that the bass is heading toward a leap,

Critical time in fighting a bass is when the fish is near the boat. If possible, stand in the boat and be ready to meet a sudden lunge, giving line by extending your arms and bending over.

Leading a bass in figure-eights at boatside prior to landing him. This prevents slack from forming in the line, one of the main causes of lost bass.

giving you time to make a move if you care to. The best move is to relax and enjoy it, since there are few spectacles as stirring as a good bass climbing for altitude.

During that jump, however, a bass has his best opportunity to rid himself of the lure, and many times he does. That being the case, if you're hungry or if you think the fish is a lunker, try to keep him from jumping. Most of the time you can keep the fish from breaking water by burying your rod and sweeping back with it just before the bass gets to the top. The lighter your line test, the bigger the bass, and the farther out he is, the less likely it is that this maneuver will succeed.

How much you control a fighting bass depends a great deal on the rod you are using. All else being equal, the longer the rod the easier it is to maintain a tight line and to maintain pressure on the fish. The fly rod is therefore a deadly weapon. It will break the back of the biggest bass in short order if there is room to play the fish. Conversely, with a short rod it is more difficult to keep the

Best way to prevent a bass from jumping and throwing the hook is to thrust rod in water and sweep backwards with it just before fish gets to surface.

line tight and more skill is required during the fight. After the fish is worked in near the boat, the advantage of a fly rod diminishes, because in such close quarters it is more awkward for most anglers to use than a rod of 5 to 7 feet.

The fight of a hooked bass is short and violent. His runs are not long, and neither is the duration of the battle. As a consequence, most bass are still lively when they are brought to the boat. A 2-pound fish—and that is a healthy average in most places—is no match for a 150-pound man and a 10-pound-test line. Thus he comes in quickly, being simply overpowered, and still has a lot of life left when boated. If you will *play* the fish for another minute or two he will usually roll over in complete exhaustion, making the landing procedure simple.

A reel is not a winch. It can be used as one by just cranking the bass in once you have him hooked, and this is acceptable if the fish is small. On a big, strong bass use the same "pumping" technique used by saltwater big-fish anglers.

Boating A Bass

Most bass are small—less than 2 pounds. With fish this size, and with sensible test line, it is perfectly practical to swing them over the side into the boat. Note that I said "swing." Bring the bass to within 1 or 2 feet of the end of the rod, get him moving toward or alongside the boat, and just ease him up over the edge. This is

Pumping technique used by saltwater anglers is effective for fighting lunkers. Fish is brought in by pulling back on rod, reeling in as rod comes forward.

where working the fish in a figure-eight pattern at boatside comes in handy. That way you can form an opinion as to how big, how vigorous, and how well hooked the fish is.

Do not lift your rod straight up to boat the bass. To do so with a fish of any size would bend a light-action rod into a "U" shape, and would be a good way to snap the tip, particularly on those with fast-tip action. Neither should you lift the bass into the boat with 4 or 5 feet of line still out.

Now for exceptions. Observe the accompanying photograph of a fisherman landing a bass. He obviously has out several feet of line and he is lifting the rod straight up. Both are proper under the circumstances. He was floating a small, fast creek where you seldom have time to use a net or to play a fish down until you can grab him by the jaw. You don't have time to work him along the boat and swing him aboard. The accepted technique in this situation is to try to turn one of the fish's jumps into the boat. This calls for a strong line and a rod with backbone, without a fast-tip action. In swift creeks all casts are short. If you hesitate, after hooking a bass, you will probably be around the next bend, and the fish will be

Most bass can be swung over the side of the boat. Do not lift the rod straight up but get the fish moving toward or alongside boat and ease him over the side.

fouled on a log or treetop before you can make use of any conventional landing technique.

Lifting a bass into the boat with the rod is not as practical when using a fly rod. I have done it, but I land most bass on a fly rod by grabbing the leader within a foot or two of the lure and swinging the fish aboard. This is the landing technique I use much of the time when casting, spinning or spincasting. It is not as foolproof as hoisting them with the rod, since your hand and arm has no "give" once you begin to swing the fish upward. A rod does, and can compensate for a sudden surge of the bass.

Next on the list of landing techniques is the classic maneuver of slipping your thumb into the mouth of the bass and grabbing him by his lower jaw. I rather like to do it, since it is such a clean, positive method, but I actually use the method less than any of the

Accepted creek-fishing method of boating a bass is to turn one of the fish's jumps to your advantage and hoist him over the side. In a swiftly moving current, there is no time to play a fish until he's ready for the net.

others. The difficulty with it is that everything must be just right. The bass must be worn down, since trying to get a thumb into his mouth if he's not is nearly impossible. His mouth must be open, since it is impossible to get a thumb in otherwise. There is also danger from the hooks of the lure when boating a bass in this manner, less with single-hooked plugs than with the multi-hooked jobs, but considerable with any of them.

By far the most efficient way to boat a bass is with a landing net. It has none of the disadvantages associated with the three previous methods. If I have a net handy, I use it without fail on big bass. I don't use a net on most small bass, say those up to 2 pounds, because I dislike getting the hooks tangled in the net. But I carry a good net at all times when fishing from a boat, because it is invaluable in landing a big bass, or in landing a bass of any size which is poorly hooked.

If your shock leader is heavy enough, and if the fish is sufficiently tired, you can land a bass by grasping the leader and lifting him over the side.

Landing a bass by grasping with the thumb inside the lower jaw. The fish must be fairly subdued for this method to work, and angler must be wary of hooks.

Classic way to land a bass is with a landing net. Submerge net in the water and when fish is subdued lead him into it head first.

A bass net should have a big, strong frame and a handle 3 to 4 feet long. The webbing should be of nylon, and the mesh should be large. Nylon is light, doesn't absorb water, and won't rot to let that lunker through at a critical time. Large mesh offers less water resistance when you are netting a fish and lessens the possibility of tangling hooks. One new development is a rubber-meshed net which increases in depth according to the size of the fish. Hooks don't tangle in it, either.

The ideal way to net a bass is to play the fish until he rolls over on his side, submerge the net and keep it still, then lead the bass into the net head first. But it seldom works out that way. If you really want to put that bass into the boat, try to net him the first time he's within reach—head first, tail first or sideways.

In very clear water bass will sometimes seek to avoid the net; therefore, keeping it motionless in the water has merit at times. Far more frequently, however, a decisive effort to "dip up" the bass with the landing net gets better results. Time and again I have seen a bass jump and throw the hook while being led slowly toward the motionless, submerged landing net held by the angler's partner. In most cases, all that was necessary to save the bass was for the netter to net the bass.

CHAPTER SIXTEEN

Skittering for Bass

THIS is a term applied to bass fishing with a cane pole and artificial lure. In your part of the country you may call it something else, but, whatever the name, it is still just a manner of presenting a lure to a bass without casting or trolling.

From the window of my house, I can see the Cane River, and on many days I can see one of the best exponents of this art in action. This elderly fellow, in his eighties, is an artist with a 12-foot cane pole, a line of the same length, and a Bomber or Hellbender plug. Those are the only two lures he uses, and he catches a lot of bass. He sits on the front seat of a 12-foot aluminum boat, which he weights at the front end with a couple of concrete building blocks to cut down wind resistance. As he eases along the shoreline his coverage, like a wading fisherman's, can best be described as thorough. I have watched him fish a brush pile many times, and it is seldom that he makes fewer than two-dozen "casts" to it. He probes in with the lure time and time again from every possible angle. His casts are amazingly accurate.

His technique is really a method of casting with a cane pole rather than with rod and reel. It has limitations, but it also has advantages. Not least among the latter is the fact that he can ease his

Expert skitterer displays his form on river in front of author's home. With a 12-foot cane pole and line of the same length, he casts gently to a brush pile. He'll work the spot from every angle.

lure into the water with scarcely a ripple. This makes the method particularly deadly when bass are in the extreme shallows, such as during the spawning season. The best lure in these instances is one of the spinner-skirt affairs—a "safety-pin" lure.

Much better known is the form of skittering which calls for a very short line on the cane pole, usually one not more than 3 feet long. With this the lure is simply lowered into the water in a likely-looking spot. The advantage here is that you can get the plug or spinner into spots where you couldn't possibly cast, and you can work it in the same spot for as long as you choose. Pull that lure back and forth beside a log, 4 feet in one direction then back again, and something drastic is apt to happen.

"Dowjacking" is another term for this type of fishing, and it originated from the use of the big Heddon topwater plug, the "Dowagiac," on a cane pole. Most popular was the model with spinners fore and aft which was armed with five sets of treble hooks. Any modern surface lure with spinners can be fished like this. The trick is to keep it moving back and forth over the bass's lair, sputtering and kicking, until the fish can stand it no longer.

A "jigging" technique is very effective and popular with skitterers. As the name indicates, the fisherman eases his lure—and this must be a sinking lure—into the water and jiggles it up and down. The combination spinner-feather-bucktail lures are good for this, as is a plain bucktail, marabou or polar-bear jig. This jigging technique is especially useful in very thick cover. Wind your line around the end of the pole until only a foot or so is left and you can work it in spots which look impossible.

Many lakes throughout the nation, especially the smaller, shallower ones which are protected from severe winds, frequently support heavy growths of aquatic vegetation. By midsummer, sizeable areas in them are difficult, if not impossible, to fish with rod and reel. In such situations, try "dunking." Take a cane pole with a 3-foot line and work every opening in the vegetation that you can find. If there is a 6-inch hole, you can lower the lure down through it.

Duckweed will frequently blanket the surface of a lake in such quantities that it is impossible to fish a lure in the normal way. Dunking is poison in such circumstances.

In addition to the skittering, jigging and dunking lures which have been mentioned before, try the new soft plastic products. I have found the plastic salamander, rigged with a heavy sinker,

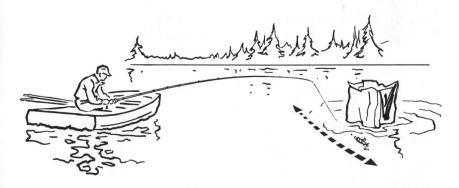

Another effective skittering technique is to use a 3-foot line and draw plug back and forth beside a stump, log or brush pile. Using a jig or plastic lure, you can dunk it into openings in weeds and jiggle it up and down.

especially good. The sinker lets you pinpoint placement of the lure more precisely, especially if any wind is blowing, and it also provides enough weight to take the lure down through a layer of grass, weeds or moss.

When you feel a bass take the salamander or plastic worm, let him pull the tip of the pole down, against very slight resistance, to the surface of the water or slightly below it. Then set the hook. You must treat it much as you would a plastic worm fished on a rod and reel.

Another exciting and often productive form of skittering is the use of an unweighted plastic worm fished on top of a heavy blanket of duckweed or other similar floating vegetation. Lower the worm gently to the surface so that it doesn't break through, then pull it slowly back and forth. A bass will see either the worm, the shadow of the worm, or the movement, and his explosive strike is a sight to behold. Many which strike will not be hooked, but the heart-stopping action is worth the price of admission. Then, too, the same bass will often try again and again if the worm is presented in a sufficiently tantalizing fashion.

Variations in offering artificials to bass by using a cane pole are almost endless. Yau can "fly cast" with one, using a line about the same length as the pole, using either popping bugs or underwater streamer-spinner combinations, and can do a pretty good job of it.

One of the most unusual versions of skittering was originated by a friend of mine, who conceived of it for a particular situation on the Little Pee Dee River in South Carolina many years ago. The

Plastic salamander should be rigged with a heavy sinker to take it straight down in brush and weeds.

water was high, out of the banks and into the woods, and bass were concentrated in flooded thickets where casting was out of the question. My ingenious friend fastened a stave from an umbrella to the tip end of a stout cane pole, leaving about half of the steel rib protruding. That half he then bent at right angles to the pole, and to the eye on the end of it he wired a River Runt. The method was to stick the end of the contraption beneath the bushes under water and then to rotate the handle of the cane pole in one direction and then in the other. The lure, in turn, described a swift half circle in each direction. Under those circumstances, the method was deadly.

For skittering I recommend a monofilament line testing at least 25 pounds. By the nature of the game, you are often fishing in the midst of trouble—limbs, logs, trees, thickets—for skittering is a shallow-fishing operation. It is at its best in shallow, debris-filled waters. The dunking technique with plastic worm or salamander is best where duckweed or other aquatic vegetation blankets the surface, because bass will lie in the shade beneath it, sheltered from the heat and light of the sun. In fact, the best periods of the day for such dunking are often the hot hours during midday.

When using a line the length of your cane pole you can actually "play" a bass unless he is an unusually big one. With the short line it is mostly a matter of sliding the pole behind you and dragging the fish in. Use a weedless lure, or a weedless hook on the plastic creations, where you think it is called for.

If you haven't tried skittering, don't ignore it. It is a lot of fun. Try it and add another technique to your repertoire of bass angling skills.

Every angler fishes with the hope that he'll land a lunker like this one.

CHAPTER SEVENTEEN

Lunkers

How big is a lunker bass? A few fishermen I know consider anything less than a 7- or 8-pounder not worth shouting about. If a fish goes below 5 pounds they don't even mention it. For many anglers, however, anything over 4 pounds ranks as a big bass. Yet most fishermen have never caught a bass that weighed more than 4 pounds. They may have fished for years and may have caught thousands of bass, but none of them were lunkers. There seems to be something about that 4-pound mark. It is a barrier which, for many, is difficult to surmount. After the first time, the crossing seems easier and the feat is accomplished more often.

Bass fishing can be thoroughly satisfying when the big one on the stringer doesn't exceed 2 pounds. With appropriate tackle even a 3-pounder speaks with authority. But the man who says that the thrill of catching a 2-pounder is as great as that of whipping a lunker just hasn't experienced the latter.

Lunker bass don't do as much cavorting on top as do the youngsters, which should come as no surprise. They just rip off line in short bursts and tugs, heading downward toward a stump or rock on which to foul the line. When you sink the hooks home in one of these monsters and feel that surge of power your heart does strange things.

Looking for Lunkers

There are many more small bass than large ones—an obvious statement, but it explains in large measure why most of the bass you catch weigh less than 2 pounds. There are other reasons, in addition to the mere numerical abundance of the smaller fish, and by examining these we will find keys to help unlock the trophy bass treasure house.

Bass grow larger and more rapidly in warmer climates than they do in colder climates. That being true, the farther south one goes in this hemisphere the better the chances are for landing lunkers. If we go too far south, we will be out of the range of smallmouth, but the world-record smallmouth was caught July 9, 1955, in Dale Hollow Lake near the Tennessee-Kentucky border by D. H. Hayes, of Leitchfield, Kentucky. It weighed 11 pounds 15 ounces. Hayes caught this fish on a trolled Bomber. Scale samples showed that the fish was 13 years old, and it was 27 inches long. When 12 years old the bass was an estimated 26 inches in length, whereas a Lake Michigan smallmouth the same age would be only 17 inches long.

Among largemouths, of course, the Florida fish so far outweigh those from the rest of the nation that most national fishing contests have a separate division for bass caught in that state. The long growing season plays its part, but I'm convinced that geographical varieties of bass exist, too.

If time and money are of no concern to you in your quest for big bass, go south or find a bass lake in a primitive area. In these primitive spots, bass have had time to grow old and heavy, and their ranks haven't been thinned and educated by anglers.

Big Bass Are Deep

All else being equal, the biggest bass in a lake will spend most of their time deeper than the other members of their species. If you are concentrating on lunkers, therefore, spend more time dredging the bottom than you do fishing surface lures or shallow runners, pleasant as these are to work with. This is important whether your lake is 10 feet deep or 100 feet deep, although obviously more so in the latter case. In the shallower ponds the lunker doesn't have to move upward very far to be within striking distance of even a topwater plug.

If you accept the fact that most bass spend most of their time on the bottom in bunches, in water deeper than 6 or 8 feet, and if you fish accordingly, you are well on your way to lunkers.

Bass on the bottom tend to group together according to size. Catch a 2-pounder and odds are good that most of those you catch there will be in that range. Catch a lunker and you may have hit the big bass jackpot. You may catch more trophy bass from that one spot in an hour than you've ever caught before in your entire life.

Lake Bistineau, in northwest Louisiana, is not noted as a big bass lake, yet several years ago an angler found a sweet spot on the bottom near the channel, and strung a limit of fifteen fish which *averaged* just a shade less than 5 pounds each. The temperature that morning was 18 degrees, and he caught them by twitching a bucktail.

If you're serious about lunker hunting, a good depth finder is one of your most valuable tools. With it you can find those deep holes in shallow lakes, and in all lakes you can find the underwater structures which attract bass: shelves, ridges and dropoffs.

Spring Fishing

All bass move to the shallows each spring to spawn, and this includes lunkers. That being the case you should fish as much as possible during that time if your laws permit it. You won't find concentrations of big fish, but this period of the year is the time when random fishing along the shoreline is most apt to produce—lunkers and otherwise.

There is a general impression among many anglers that the female bass are the bigger, but studies have indicated that there is little if any difference in growth rates of the two sexes. During this spawning season, of course, females will look bigger and weigh more, before they spawn, because of the eggs they are carrying.

Lines for Lunkers

The line you're using is too light! I can hear many of you reply, "He doesn't even know what test line I use."

I know what test most bass fishermen use, and that *is* too light if you're serious about catching big bass. Looking for a lunker is like a hunt for a Boone and Crockett bighorn. Opportunities at a record, in either case, are few and far between and you don't want to miss when they arrive.

I recently polled an array of the finest lunker-busting talent in the country, and the tabulated data shows that half of them use 20-pound-test line most of the time. Very few ever go below 15-pound test.

Baby your line. Remember that any knot decreases the strength of a line somewhat, and some knots can chop the effective test in half. Use the good ones and tie them carefully each time. If you fish a whole day without retying your lure to your line several times, shame on you. The flexing of the line near the lure, which occurs when you cast, wears and weakens it.

Get in the habit of running your fingers up and down the line for several feet near the lure. You will frequently notice little nicks—especially in monofilament—which are signals that you should chop that portion off and retie. Abrasion of the line on the jaw of a bass, which is particularly prevalent when a bass is hooked with the lure entirely inside his mouth (as often happens with worms and eels), will weaken a line and calls for remedial action.

Big bass are tough. Their jaws are strong and hard to penetrate with a hook. Couple that with the fact that they are most often found on the bottom in deep water, and it is obvious that enthusiastic performance is necessary to set the hook in these bruisers. The strike required to sink the steel home under these conditions would break a light line.

It is difficult to break a moderate test line by smoothly sweeping back with your rod, holding it at approximately right angles to the line, no matter how much pressure you put on it, but it takes more than this to positively set the hook in a big bass down deep. A big bass will often have the entire lure—and we're talking here about either the jig and worm or the jig and eel—inside his mouth when you try to set the hook. If he just clamps down tight a smooth strike by the fisherman may move the bass, but it doesn't move the lure inside his mouth and therefore doesn't set the hook. You can demonstrate this by completely enclosing a hook-studded

By portaging into a backwoods lake in Florida, the author and his companions find lunker water which hasn't been overfished.

plug in your fist, and holding on tightly while somebody pulls on the line attached to that plug. As long as the pull is smooth and you hold tight, the hooks will not hurt you at all.

Lunker Lures

Any lure will catch a big bass now and then. Some huge bass have been taken on fly-rod popping bugs. The most outlandish creation which formerly had no status as a bass catcher will sometimes intrigue a lunker—perhaps because it *is* so outlandish.

Some lures have a justly earned reputation as being big bass killers. Heading this list is the weighted plastic worm and the black pork eel fished on a bucktail jig. Neither of these combinations is much more than a decade old, which makes their heady status all the more remarkable.

Homer Circle, certainly one of the best and most knowledgeable bass fishermen in the nation, says that the long strip of pork was being used as a bass lure in Georgia as long as three decades ago, but it was not until the early to mid-fifties that somebody dyed it black. When that happened the black eel became one of the deadliest of bass lures.

Two other great lunker lures are the Bomber and the Hellbender. Floaters when at rest, deep divers on the retrieve, this pair of Texas-bred plugs have accounted for a vast number of lunker bass. The world-record smallmouth was taken on the Bomber, and the world-record spotted bass on the Hellbender.

The bigger Spoonplugs, although fished by fewer anglers than either the Bomber or Hellbender, must be listed in the same group as bottom-walking big-bass killers.

All three are excellent trolling as well as casting lures, and in the huge open reservoirs which are dominating today's bass-fishing picture, trolling may be the easiest way for the average angler to catch a lunker. A short, stiff rod and heavy monofilament line is the best rig for trolling. Experiment with running your outboard at various speeds and trolling your lure at various distances behind your boat. Troll parallel to the shoreline and vary your distance from it, but when you work across points give them a thorough criss-crossing back and forth several times before moving on.

Skillful anglers Jody Grigg, left, and Carl Piersall display a string holding more lunkers than most bass fishermen catch in a lifetime.

Your objective when trolling should be to keep the lure running just above the lake bottom, tipping it now and then. When you do hit a bass trolling—STOP! Fish that area for at least fifteen minutes, preferably by casting, but by trolling if necessary to get your lure down.

A good policy when you catch a bass on the trolled lure is to sink a black eel or weighted worm down at that spot to see what happens.

Surface lures which are noted lunker plugs include the Zara Spook, Injured Minnow, Lucky 13, Darter, Dalton Special, Chugger, Jitterbug and Bass-Oreno.

The Johnson Silver Minnow, armed with a pork rind, has earned for itself a firm place in the hearts of lunker specialists, especially in Florida.

The safety-pin lures, the spinner-skirt affairs, take many trophy bass, particularly when they are used for ledge-hopping and bottom-bumping.

Here is another lunker development worth noting. On Bull Shoals Lake in northern Arkansas and southern Missouri, Sam Welch reported on lunker bass catches—those over 4 pounds—from 1955 through 1965. In 402 weeks of reporting during those eleven years he tallied 39,860 lunkers from 4 pounds to over 13, and recorded what they were caught on.

In 1965, for the first time, surface lures accounted for more lunkers than did any other category. He attributes it to the popularity and effectiveness of the Rapala-type plugs.

There are many, many excellent bass lures which I have not mentioned here, of course, but these are the ones which have earned the reputation of taking more than their share of lunkers.

CHAPTER EIGHTEEN

Think Bass

W<small>HEN</small> I pass a stream or lake along the highway, my mind starts musing along these lines: "That narrow point just below the cabin probably points to a whole batch of bass offshore. Bet most people don't notice that it starts to dogleg just before it hits the water . . . Look at the way that creek eddies around the bridge pilings. Can't you just see a jig and eel sunk down beside them? . . . And that hole where the creek bends down below. Hmmm, flip that worm in at the head of it with just a bit of sinker and let the current carry in and in and down . . . Boy, that's typical! Look at that guy plugging the shoreline, in the middle of the summer and two hours after sunup. If he catches two bass he'll be lucky."

Having had long practice, I can usually manage to carry on a fair conversation with anybody who happens to be riding with me, but I do slip now and then. It's a bit embarrassing when my wife asks, "Did the boys tell you what happened at school yesterday?" and I answer, "Yes, they should be moving to the shallows in a few days."

But she understands, since she sometimes answers my query as to what's for supper with, "A purple worm in those treetops should be poison."

We think bass!

It is not necessary to have this affliction in order to be a good bass fisherman, but it definitely is necessary for you to think bass when you go bass fishing. Unless you do, there will be vast periods of time when you might just as well be back home as far as catching fish is concerned.

A positive frame of mind makes for a more successful bass fisherman. Continually keep in mind that you *will* find the fish, that you *will* establish the pattern, and that you *will* have caught bass before your trip is ended. At times you won't but such a mental attitude helps you to keep your mind on the business at hand.

Business, did I say? Catching bass isn't all there is to bass fishing, of course. If a man would rather commune with nature in an absent-minded fashion than work at catching bass, fine and dandy. Lakes are filled with fishermen like that, and the nation is better off for it. They may enjoy their outing even more than I do mine.

I, too, am extremely fond of communing with nature, but it just so happens that I commune better if I have a fish on, and this *is* a book about how to catch bass.

"You sure do confidence that bait," an old paddler told me once when I tied on a battle-scarred favorite lure. He had succinctly pinpointed one of the essential ingredients of successful bass fishing.

You must "confidence" your actions when fishing. If you doubt the effectiveness of your lure, you won't fish it as well. For you it *won't* be as effective. If you doubt the wisdom of the method of fishing at the time—water depth or what have you, odds are good that the procedure *is* wrong for you.

There are exceptions to this as to all generalities. All of us know of instances where desperation tactics, in which the angler had little faith, paid off, but they are exceptions.

If you "think bass" you will learn from every experience. You will retain the bits and pieces of which excellence is composed. You will observe and hear facts which escape notice of the absent-minded angler, and you will remember them because your desire to do so is great.

You will notice and remember the places in a lake where you catch bass. When you fish with a friend or a guide, you'll make a mental record of how they approach bass fishing in that particular lake or stream. You'll file for future reference information as to exactly where they take you to fish, whether you happen to catch bass at all of the spots, or not; what lures they use and how they rig them; and how they fish those lures.

If you overhear bits of bass-fishing gossip from the next booth at your local coffee house, you eavesdrop. If you see a group of bass fishermen talking on the dock, you eavesdrop. If the situation permits, or if eavesdropping won't get the job done, go directly to your potential source of information and ask, "Do you mind if I listen? I've never seen such a string of bass. This is a new lake to me. You've sure got a neat way of rigging that boat. You say you trolled a plastic worm—never heard of that."

Flattery will get you everywhere!

One of the above approaches, or something similar to fit the occasion, will usually open the gate, and you cannot afford to pass up any possible source of bass-fishing information which could add to your angling effectiveness. Now you're thinking bass.

Fish with as many different bass fishermen, preferably in their backyard lake where they are at home, as you possibly can. From all of them you can learn something, and intelligent observation of *good* bass fishermen in action is one of the fastest shortcuts to success on your own. Intelligent observation, that is. Many who are exposed never learn more than "what he caught 'em on."

Don't be afraid to ask why your partner or guide is fishing the way he's fishing and where he's fishing. Many times the answer will simply be that such tactics and a particular lure got results in that same spot on earlier occasions, but sometimes there will be a more definite reason which you can tuck away in your mental bass-fishing file.

Anglers who think bass can, and usually do, develop the mechanics of angling to a fine point. They become highly skilled at casting, at boat handling, at netting a bass or "thumbing" a bass, at tying knots, at operating an outboard, at pulling a boat trailer. They also become highly adept in areas where something other than mechanical skill takes over. They get a "feel" for things.

I can "feel" it quite often when a bass makes a pass at my lure even when he never touches it, yet I still remember my disbelief when I first heard a fisherman say that. "One rolled at it," was the way he put it when he lifted the lure from the water and fired it back to the same place. "I'll get him this time."

He did, and I've done the same thing many times since then. Fishing an underwater lure which you retrieve by reeling, as opposed to one which you bump, crawl or yo-yo along the bottom, you can actually detect a break in the rhythm of the lure if a bass makes a pass at it but veers away without striking. It is quite an advantage to know that a bass is *there* and probably willing.

Such finesse requires concentration, and requires that the angler be aware that this is possible. He must be familiar with and sensitive to the feel of the lure being used, otherwise he can't possibly know when a swirl of water down below has momentarily disrupted its normal action.

Expert bass fishermen acquire a "feel" for bass water. They learn to read it. Perhaps it's a culmination of years of experience, but many of them almost seem to know when they're going to catch a bass.

I asked some of these experts the following question: "What is the most important single factor in successful bass fishing?"

Here are some of their answers:

Desire

Determination

Persistence

Patience

Keeping the plug working

Stamina

Concentration

These answers recurred again and again from anglers in many parts of the country. If you want to be a better fisherman, take them to heart.

Think bass!

CHAPTER NINETEEN

Fish, Fish and Fish Again

IF an angler fished 10 times last year and caught 15 bass, how many bass will he catch this year if he fishes 100 times?

The answer is 150 bass. Right?

WRONG!!

A better answer would be 300, or 500 or even 1500, for it is a fact that angling success for a bass fisherman tends to increase in geometric rather than in arithmetic fashion in accord with the number of trips he makes. The more he fishes, the higher will be his average catch per trip.

There are a number of reasons why this is true, and they are easy to understand.

First and most important, the more you go fishing the more times you are apt to hit the "hot" periods. Your chances of being on the lake with lure in the water when the bass are in available locations and willing to strike increase proportionately with an increase in the number of trips you make. Each additional time you "hit 'em right" you catch a bundle of bass.

As stressed in the previous chapter, persistence and stamina are two of the most valuable qualities a bass fisherman can possess. This means that much time is often required on an outing before you find the fish and establish the pattern. Most or all of a full day can be utilized in accomplishing this (provided that you can do it at all on that day), and it is a fact that most bass fishermen will not work at it that extensively. That is why *frequent* trips are important. They increase the probability of the angler hitting the fish on those half-day trips.

In this connection let me emphasize one point: the middle of the day can be one of the most productive bass-fishing times of all. Many anglers have a habit of discarding the mid-day hours, say from 10:00 until 2:00, or even from 11:00 until 1:00, and oftentimes they have discarded their best chance to catch bass. If you can fish only half a day, try to stretch it to include that noon period at one end of your trip or the other. You may not care to fish strenuously over a protracted period of time, say from daybreak until 1:00 P.M., and there are certainly times and places when I am in that frame of mind. When that happens I try to spend the time I care to allot to bass fishing within the hours I think are the most productive.

Let's take an example. If I can fish only four hours in a morning, here is the way I am apt to program it. I'll be on the lake and *fishing* when daybreak arrives and I'll fish for a couple of hours. The other two I'll allot to the noon period. In the early session I may quit a half hour early or so if action is slow, or I may stretch it if fish are hitting. The noon period gets what is left.

Daybreak is not the same as sunrise. If you leave the dock about the time of official sunrise you probably won't get down to effective fishing until half an hour later. Since there is enough light for you to begin fishing a half hour *before* daylight, you will have lost an hour of fishing at a time when angling is often very productive. If you are usually guilty of a late start, and want to add several bass to your average stringer, get going an hour earlier.

Second most important as a reason for the geometric increase in bass caught is that frequent trips enable the angler to keep up with the fish. If he could go every day his task of finding the fish and of establishing the pattern would be tremendously simplified. That pattern and the location of the fish *can* change drastically overnight, but generally they remain the same. The odds are in your favor today, therefore, if you found them and caught them yesterday, because experimenting with various locations, tactics and lures will be held to a minimum.

In the spring, when bass begin moving from deep water toward the shallows to spawn, they frequently do it in stages. One week they may be in 40-foot water, the next in 30-foot water, and so on until they reach spawning depth. The angler who is able to be afloat regularly during this time has a great advantage over the one who can fish only two or three times a month.

Frequent fishing keeps an angler sharp—both physically and mentally. As with any activity which requires physical skill, coordination and awareness, practice will get you nearer to perfect. The more you handle rod, reel, lines, boat, stringer, anchor, lures, paddle, outboard motor, net and knife, the more adept you become at using them.

One of the first indications that I'm rusty is failure to watch my line. In lakes where I fish a great deal accuracy in casting is very important, but an angler can be accurate at placing the lure yet still stay fouled up much of the time. This happens because any breeze will drift a light line from the clear course of the lure off to one side, often around a stump or limb.

When I'm sharp I snub the line down near the end of the cast so that it hits the water quickly and in a straight line. After a few weeks layoff, however, I find myself forgetting to feather or thumb, an action which becomes almost automatic if I'm fishing frequently enough.

Little things like tying a knot in flimsy mono give me more trouble if I'm fishing infrequently, and I'm sure I don't tie them quite as well under such conditions. When I return to bass fishing after less important things have occupied me for a few weeks, I find that my casts don't land exactly where and how they should, none of my gear seems to be in just the right place at the right time, and I catch fewer fish because of it.

To catch bass consistently you must THINK about your fishing. If you are regularly using the plans of attack which you know will catch bass, they readily come to mind while you're fishing. You do what you should do almost instinctively.

If weeks elapse between fishing trips, however, each time you hit the water you must make a conscious effort to find the fish and establish the pattern. You become mentally lazy if you aren't careful, and one of the first signs that you're in that rut is that you prolong an unproductive tactic too long. It is utterly foolish to continue to do the same thing after you have spent a reasonable length of time proving that it isn't catching fish. If, for instance, you work the very shallow water along a certain stretch of shoreline for half an hour, or even an hour, and get no action, do something else. You have evaluated that particular area, found it wanting, so try another. Frequent fishing keeps your mind attuned to these points, and it in turn insists that you use your time afloat to best advantage.

Keep Your Gear in Shape

A friend of mine had a sudden opportunity to fish after a piscatorial lapse of several months. A report that bass were hitting on a nearby lake, plus an overly frustrating day at the office, triggered him into action, but the results were far from satisfying.

Enroute to the lake he noticed his boat trailer was swaying badly, discovered that one tire was almost flat, so he had to creep the remaining distance. Once afloat he found that the boat battery was dead, so he had to crank the big outboard by hand and was unable to use his electric motor. With a fairly brisk breeze blowing, he got plenty of paddling exercise before the afternoon was over.

Our hero next discovered that his favorite rod had a broken guide, and remembered that he had failed to replace the line on his spinning reel. It had become twisted on his last outing, months earlier, and had taken a "set" in that twisted position. As a crowning blow, the top on his only jar of pork rind was rusted fast, and he had to break the jar to get at the contents.

He did catch a few bass, but it is not a trip he remembers with a great deal of pleasure. It is unlikely that you will ever encounter such a bizarre series of unfortunate episodes, but any *one* can ruin your fishing trip and reduce your catch to nothing.

The more you fish the more you become mindful of your equipment. You just naturally are more inclined to see that your outboard is running properly, that your boat is equipped with landing net, paddles, gasoline can, spare shear pins, flashlight, running lights and life preservers. I've seen each of those items left behind.

Reading books will help teach you the methodology of bass fishing, but you catch bass only by going bass fishing, and going again and again. Just fishing for bass more frequently will insure that you will catch many more fish than you now do, but to get maximum benefit from your extensive exposure afloat, keep a notebook. You will find it impossible to remember all that you want to remember without some kind of written reminder, about where you fished, when you fished, how you fished, who you fished with and what you caught.

Take the bottom sanctuaries, the worm holes, the schooling spots—places where bass congregate with regularity to the exclusion of most of the rest of the lake. You just can't remember all of them if you fish often. This is particularly true if you fish more than one lake. Make a record in your notebook of these spots, even to the point of sketching landmarks by which you can recognize them, and you will be able to pinpoint these locations.

Just that much is a tremendous help, but if you can go a step beyond, your experience will be even more valuable. That step is to record the conditions under which you meet with success at any particular lake. Those conditions would include: date, lake, place in lake where you caught them, air and water temperature, water level, time of day, condition of barometer, moon phase and the lure and technique you used to catch the fish.

Most bass fishermen won't care to be this meticulous about their angling. I don't always make the notes about my trips which I would like to, usually because I just don't take time to do so. If you will do it, however, and will jot down the little tricks and techniques which you learn from each good bass fisherman with whom you share a boat, your stringer will become heavier as the years go by.

CHAPTER TWENTY

Fish the Hot Lakes

ANGLERS in most areas of the nation have the option of fishing one or more lakes which furnish abnormally good bass fishing, or of fishing others where the bass fishing is not as good for the average fisherman. Strange as it may seem, many of them elect to fish the lakes where they have been least successful.

The quality of bass fishing in natural lakes and streams changes over the years as various ecological factors play their part. The fishing seems to go in cycles for no explicable reason.

But many natural lakes and streams are taking a back seat to the man-made reservoirs, which now provide one-third of all the angling in the nation, and which will furnish an ever-increasing percentage for the foreseeable future. Never before in history have so many lakes been under construction. Dams have been built in all parts of the nation for water conservation, hydroelectric power, flood-control and recreation.

Significant to you as a bass fisherman is the fact that we can predict with accuracy just what the bass-fishing potential of a lake will be even before the dam is built. It is a well-known fact that man-made reservoirs follow a rather fixed pattern of fishing productivity. Fantastic spawning success is the rule as newly impounded waters spread over virgin ground, and fishing improves so rapidly it seems impossible. Within a year or two, from a standing start, most new lakes are swarming with bass.

As the years pass, the productivity of a reservoir declines. The lake is actually settling down to normal, according to fisheries biologists, who insist that the initial burst of phenomenal angling is abnormal. This tapering off may begin in as little as five years after impoundment, but it's usually closer to ten.

The decline in productivity is attributed to a number of causes, among them nitrogen deficiency in the soil, the overtaking of game-fish populations by nongame species, and that repressive factor discussed in the chapter on management. Some insist that the bass become educated to lures and fishermen, and that once the easily harvested segment of the bass population is removed fishing becomes poorer. But the answers to all reservoir fisheries problems aren't known, and that's why the United States Fish and Wildlife Service is now in the midst of a research project designed to find them. Until they do, however, bass fishermen should take advantage of the knowledge we do have, that the first five or ten years in the life of a lake are often the very best of all. Fish these lakes when they are hot.

In fishing these new reservoirs the angler has at least two significant things going for him. First is that the lake is filled with bass which are healthy and growing, which means that they are rambunctious and willing to do battle. The second is that the bass are unsophisticated.

Missouri fisheries biologists made a study recently in which they placed bass from heavily fished waters and from unfished waters in the same pond. Then they fished the pond with artificials during fall and spring, and the results were significant. They caught *twice as many bass* that had originated from the unfished waters.

I usually consider a lake as getting into the hot stage in about its third year. For a year or two before that fishing will be good, but the multitude of bass will be in the 1- or 2-pound class at best. After about three years, bass are plentiful, but many are also big enough—3 to 5 pounds—to get your attention when they hit.

The length of time before bass fishing in a lake begins to taper off varies considerably. Most often it occurs between the fifth and tenth year following impoundment, but rarely as late as the twelfth or fifteenth year.

The phenomenal few years of fishing in the early life of a reservoir is a reasonable facsimile of the regular brand of angling experienced in the overflow areas of the deep South. In these overflows, vast areas of hardwood bottomland are left high and dry much of the year, but then are inundated when flood waters seek their way to the sea in late winter and early spring. When this occurs, the fish in the permanent pools and streams of the overflow country surge out into the newly flooded land. They find living space and food conditions superb, and spawning success and growth rates are fantastic. The diluting effect of huge quantities of fresh water, say the biologists, eliminates the "birth control" effect of the repressive factor.

Periodic drawdowns in some reservoirs have created artificial overflow situations, sometimes intentionally to benefit fishing, and sometimes by accident to achieve some other desired result. This often has the effect of prolonging the hot stage of that impoundment, indicating that it is the most practical and effective management technique for these big man-made lakes.

To be effective at increasing bass populations, of course, a lake drawdown must be timed properly. If it occurs just after spawning has taken place, results will naturally be catastrophic for that year-class. Destruction of eggs can be the *object* of a drawdown, on the other hand, if the eggs are of fish species which are in competition with bass, and which are laid at a different time of spring.

The normal pattern of operation of flood-control reservoirs is generally favorable to bass. It calls for a fall and winter drawdown to partially empty the reservoir, to ready it for the flow of late winter and spring flood waters. Where hydroelectric production is sufficiently important, or where the storage of water for domestic, irrigation or industrial use is the dominant factor, release of water from an impoundment at the proper time and in proper quantity to affect bass fishing is not usually possible.

Many governmental agencies build dams for a variety of purposes, but the leading dam builder of them all is the U. S. Army Corps of Engineers. It now, for instance, has recreational improvements at some 300 of its reservoirs across the nation. More are on the way. The 1965 budget of the Corps included funds for beginning or continuing the construction of eighty-three more reservoirs. Hundreds more have already been authorized by Congress but have yet to be financed. Additional hundreds, which may or may not be built, are already on the planning maps.

State governments have also built hundreds of lakes and are building more of them. One king-sized example of this is Toledo Bend, a joint project of the states of Louisiana and Texas, which will impound more than 180,000 acres along the Sabine River. It will be completed in 1967.

Private industry builds lakes for various reasons. Bussey Brake, in Louisiana, was built by a paper mill for water supply.

The entire point of this chapter is to emphasize that, on each of these new lakes, you can expect several years of phenomenal bass fishing. It may last for three or four years, or for ten or more,

This is the way many man-made reservoirs look at the time of the hot stage, provided trees haven't been cleared prior to impounding. Water has killed the timber, but not enough time has passed for the trees to fall and disappear.

but the important point is to take advantage of these productive peaks.

Because bass lakes do change in productivity as the years go by, a guide to the best bass fishing spots in the nation has limited value unless it is revised frequently. You can just about create your own guide, sight unseen, by listing the impoundment dates of new reservoirs. Make notes of lakes in your area, and plot your fishing accordingly. Get a list of the lakes already constructed, with the estimated completion date of each, and resolve to check them when they're about three years old. Write to the construction agencies listed above—federal, state and industrial—and ask for a list of reservoirs which are either under construction or in the planning stage.

As a reservoir ages, and bass fishing for most anglers becomes poorer, it is a sign that the bass population is settling down to a fixed routine of deep-water sanctuary areas, established migration routes, with little time spent in the shallow water. A goodly segment of the bass population has grown to be big, and the bigger the bass the tighter they school, and the less they are inclined to move into water shallow enough for the casual angler to reach them.

If you have fished this lake during its hot stage you have the advantage of knowing your waters by the time fishing begins to taper off. That being the case, it is probable that you will continue to catch strings of good fish from it.

There is some danger in this familiarity with a lake. Too many fishermen keep returning to the old fishing hole because it *is* familiar, and by doing so they frequently miss out on the superb angling at a nearby lake in its hot stage. Resist that temptation.

It is very probable that you now have, right in your fishing area, a lake which is going through this spectacular period. By the time it tapers off there will probably be others, so that by swapping your patronage from one to the other your bass-fishing prospects can be excellent from now on.

CHAPTER TWENTY-ONE

Weather

$\mathbf{T}$oo hot. Too cold. Too windy. Too calm. Too early. Too late. Too bright. Too dark. Too much rain. Not enough rain. Barometer falling. Barometer rising. Barometer high. Barometer low. Barometer steady. Barometer changing. East wind. West wind. North wind. South wind.

If you have never heard those excuses for bass failing to cooperate, it must be because you weren't listening. There are many others, but these are the ones associated with weather, and they are the most frequent alibis . . . or explanations, if you prefer.

Temperature

Air temperature sometimes gets too hot or too cold for the angler, but never for bass. One of the greatest string of bass ever taken around my area was a limit of fifteen which averaged just an ounce less than five pounds each. On the morning they were taken, the temperature was 18 degrees and ice was forming on rod and reel.

On that same lake some of the best school bass fishing takes place during the hottest months of the year, and during the hottest parts of the day. In mid-afternoon, with the water surface so placid that you can see heat waves steaming from it, or think you can, packs of bass will erupt in a feeding frenzy.

Water has excellent insulating properties when there is enough of it, therefore the bass's habitat protects him from extreme or rapid temperature changes. The air temperature can be 100 degrees or more, but most lakes exposed to that heat will still offer temperature conditions to the liking of bass.

Slight temperature variations mean a lot to fish, which is something difficult for people to understand. The heat-control mechanism of warm-blooded animals compensates for temperature changes, but cold-blooded creatures like the bass have no such provision. Their bodies conform to the temperature of the water they're in.

A few degrees of change in the body temperature of a person is an indication that he is ill. Fish aren't that sensitive, but it is reasonable to assume that bass will do what they can to keep their body temperature range where it is most comfortable, and they can control it *only* by staying in water of the right temperature.

There's a key to help fill stringers. Bass will generally try to stay in water of the temperature they prefer, which most often is quoted as being from 65 to 75 degrees F. Most experience indicates that the middle of that range, say from 68 to 72, offers the most promise most of the time—if that range is available to fish.

You can locate that temperature level with a water thermometer and a string, with the string marked at intervals so that you will know the depth you're checking. A much quicker method, albeit more expensive, is the use of an electronic thermometer. With it the temperature can be immediately read from a meter without the necessity of raising the instrument.

One of the best of these electronic hydrographic thermometers is the FT-3, manufactured by Applied Research Associates, P.O. Box 9406, Austin, Texas. It is accurate to 1 degree and to 1500 feet, weighs just over 1 pound, and is priced at $55. With it you use a hydrographic probe, which comes with a marked cable of various lengths, with cost of the probe and cable varying from $21 for a 50-foot cable to $150 for a 150-foot cable.

The advantage of a unit like this is that you can read the temperatures directly as you gradually lower the probe to the bottom. Since water temperature may change abruptly at a particular

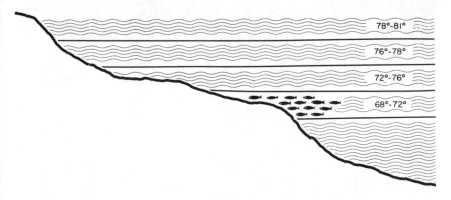

78°-81°

76°-78°

72°-76°

68°-72°

Bass seek water with a temperature range of from 68 to 72 degrees, in conjunction with bottom structures such as drop-offs. The angler's job, then, is to locate bottom structures at a depth where the water is at this range.

level, and often does, to find it with thermometer and string requires frequent trips up and down.

The depth level which water of a particular temperature assumes in a lake is rather peculiar, because the physical properties of water are themselves peculiar. The rule for any solid or liquid is that it contracts as it is cooled, and therefore becomes more dense—heavier. Water follows this pattern, but with a peculiar reversal at the temperature of 39.1 degrees F. Cooled below that point water, instead of continuing to contract and become more dense, begins to expand and become less dense. To put it simply, water is heaviest at a temperature of 39.1 degrees F.

As air temperatures fall with the coming of winter, the surface layer of water in a lake cools with it, but, being heavier, that cooler water immediately sinks. If the water temperature ever reaches that 39.1-degree mark, however, it reverses the procedure and rises to the top of the lake. Below that temperature the coldest water is at the surface, which is why ice forms *on top* of a lake or stream.

Regardless of the air temperature, then, bass are rarely subjected to water temperatures much lower than 39 degrees or much higher than about 80 degrees.

Remember that the temperature of the bass itself can be greater than that of the water *immediately* surrounding it, if affected by

Electronic thermometer is convenient and fast to use, giving a direct temperature reading continuously as the probe is lowered.

absorption from radiated sunlight. How much effect this has depends a great deal upon the clarity of the water, which varies tremendously. A light measuring device (Secchi disk) lowered in some lakes will disappear within a few inches, while in Crater Lake, Oregon, it can be seen at about 131 feet down.

Here's a sample procedure for correlating water temperature with bass. In deep water lower your thermometer until you find where the temperature *first* becomes ideal for bass (let's use 70 degrees as a norm), and note at what depth that occurs. Then move to areas of the lake where the water is about that deep, and fish on the bottom.

Bass, remember, prefer to stay ON the bottom when they're below 8 or 10 feet, therefore when you locate a bottom which has the desired temperature range you should be in business. Remember, too, that bass prefer structure with their bottom, so look for reefs, bars or ridges which are the right depth for the right temperature at the time you are fishing. Often this is not an exact thing at all, since there may be a broad band of water which has the temperature range which bass prefer.

The ultimate method of locating a starting point for your search for fish, particularly in big, deep lakes, is to find the right temperature-depth with an electronic thermometer, and then to use a sonar-type depth finder such as the Fish Lo-K-Tor to find areas of the lake which have that depth, and particularly to find bottom structure at that depth.

Wind

I dislike to bass fish when the wind is strong, but that is a personal idiosyncracy which relates only to physical discomfort. It has nothing to do with how wind affects the fish. A moderate breeze, on the other hand, can make for much more comfortable fishing when the weather is hot.

"They hit better when there's a ripple on the water," is a common saying. It could be true because: 1) the wind causing that ripple is putting more oxygen into the water, causing greater bass activity; 2) the ripple makes it more difficult for the fish to see the angler; or 3) the ripple cuts down light penetration into the water, causing bass to move upward where they're more available.

As for wind direction, of the expert fishermen I polled around the nation who think that wind direction does matter, all except one believe that some variety of east wind (NE, E, SE) is the worst possible and that some variety of west wind (NW, W, SW) is the best. The one exception thinks north is worst and south is best. Many successful bass fishermen, however, believe that wind direction is not important at all.

Wind from the east, in this hemisphere, is usually the forerunner of bad weather, which affects fishermen more than it does bass. I have experienced some of my worst bass fishing, sometimes catching not a single fish, during the cold, bright, calm days immediately following a severe cold front. In very deep lakes the bass may go deep under such conditions, beyond the workable reach of anglers. I have gone fishless at such times, however, in lakes where the maximum depth is not over 15 feet and which I covered with every variety of bottom-bumping lure.

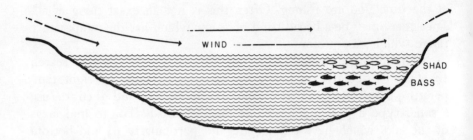

In lakes where shad are the main forage fish for bass, wind often drives the shad to the windward side. Bass congregate below them, facing into the wind.

In lakes where shad is the predominant forage fish for bass, strong winds may affect the location of bass by moving the shad from one side to the other. Look for shad on the windward side, and for bass to be down below them.

If the wind is quite strong, a lure fished *into* the wind on these windward shores may be more effective than one fished with the wind. The reason is that bass will face into the wind, so a lure coming from that direction is more noticeable to them than one coming from behind. Bass will head into the wind because the food is blown toward them from that direction; and then can maintain their position in the water, without being washed on shore, more easily by facing into the waves and water movement.

Moon

For many years hunters and fishermen have been planning their outings to be afield "when the moon is right"—meaning the times when the moon is overhead or very low in the sky. Working from this idea, John Alden Knight evolved a schedule of Major and Minor activity periods for wildlife, called them collectively the "Solunar Periods," and published the first edition of the "Solunar Tables" more than three decades ago.

As evidence that many, many fishermen believe in them, consider that they are now published daily or weekly in more than 140 newspapers throughout the United States and Canada, and that they have been published in seven foreign languages.

A good day for bass fishing—an overcast sky and a ripple on the water.

There is no denying the fact that fish do have periods when they are very active, and much greater periods when they are not very active. Whether or not these coincide with Knight's "Periods," or with any other moon-oriented system, is another matter.

About two-thirds of the excellent bass fishermen I know believe in the Solunar Tables. The other third does not. A few believe that moon phases affect fishing, but not precisely according to the schedule which Knight worked out.

Since the lunar day is slightly more than twenty-four hours and fifty minutes in length, compared with twenty-four hours for a "day" as we usually think of it, the "periods" of wildlife activity under any lunar system will change by about 50 minutes each day. Thus Knight's Major and Minor stretches progress by that fifty minutes each day.

All else being equal, I think that fishing in accord with the Solunar Periods is worth while. I keep a copy of Knight's *Field Book* for the current year, in which the Periods for that year are listed, and refer to it frequently. The book has added value because it contains places for the recording of data on fishing trips, so you can keep a log of your own activities and the conditions under which you met with or missed success. The *Field Book* is available directly from Knight at Box 208, Williamsport, Pennsylvania.

To repeat, I follow the Solunar Tables if it fits my schedule and if it seems appropriate in view of the overall situation. The fact is, all else is *not* equal many times. It is this condition, where other factors override the normal moon phase feeding periods, which leads to such a wide diversity of opinion as to their validity even among excellent bass fishermen.

Barometer

I have caught bass when the barometer was high, low, falling and rising, but it is true that atmospheric pressure does affect bass activity.

Bass fishing is usually best when the barometer is moderately high, or when it is rising regardless of where it is. Fishing can be excellent when the barometer is low, in other words, if it is rising.

Bass can feed ravenously, to the delight of anglers, during a short period after the barometer begins to drop. This is probably a feeding splurge by the fish in preparation for the bad weather which a lowering atmospheric pressure precedes.

Rain

I have never known rain to adversely affect bass fishing. If it is a cold rain accompanying a front it can lower the water temperature and move bass down, and the fish may not strike because of that lowering barometer which goes with such conditions.

A warm spring or summer rain, on the other hand, is most often beneficial to bass fishing. A warm rain in the spring, especially, when lake waters are still cool, often triggers off a superb fishing spree.

Atmospheric Conditions

Cloud cover or its absence is one of the most important factors in determining how good bass fishing will be on a particular day. Fishing is best, by far, when the sky is overcast. It is poorest when the sun shines brightest.

As in all else about bass fishing, there are execeptions here. I know of a few spots where fishing seems to be generally better when the sky is bright, and there have been occasions on every lake or stream I've ever fished extensively when we tore 'em up while the sun shone. But day in and day out, north or south, east or west, you will catch more bass when the light intensity is lowest.

Weather or Not

You positively will not catch bass if you stay at home because the wind is from the east, because you can't be out during the right moon period, because the barometer is falling, because it's too bright, or because it's raining. If you can align all the factors to your choosing, fine and dandy. Do it and be happy. If you can't, go fishing anyway.

Foul weather gear should be a part of your equipment on every trip. There are excellent rain suits and parkas available now which are completely water and windproof, which fold or roll into a small package, and which are extremely durable. This is one instance where the most inexpensive outfit you can buy can be the most expensive in the long run. Cheap rain suits are invariably inferior in quality, are styled "tight" to save material and are abominable to fish in, and frequently crack from lengthy exposure to folding and heat. Excellent rain suits are made by Charles Ulmer, Inc. and by Hodgeman. I use the Ulmer two-piece suit and the Hodgeman nylon "fishing shirt" (which comes down below the knees).

If there is any possibility of cold weather, make sure you have along warm clothing, including footgear. I use boat sneakers for fishing during the hot months, but much of the year I fish in short, insulated rubber boots.

If you are the type who is apt to get so hungry he just has to eat now and then, take along snacks of some kind so that you won't have to come off the lake at any certain time. If you've fished all morning and haven't caught fish, keep fishing until at least 1:00 P.M. And if·the fish are hitting, *never* leave until they stop. Make any excuses necessary to justify getting back late, but stay with it when you're in bass.

When you do find the fish and establish the pattern, get that fish in quickly, put him on a stringer or in the cooler, and get your lure working again. The average length of a solunar period may be from one to two hours, but I assure you that fifteen minutes will often be the difference between success and failure.

CHAPTER TWENTY-TWO

From Pond to Platter

Accuse me of bias if you will, but for table fare I prefer bass to all other freshwater fish. I smirk just a bit whenever I hear somebody say that the bass is a lot of fun to catch, but . . .

If you like to eat fish yet are not fond of bass, you are probably stubbing your toe somewhere between the pond and the platter. For how you handle that bass between the time you catch him and the time you eat him can make the difference between a gastronomic delight and an epicurean nightmare.

First, what do you do with the bass when you catch him? Practical choices are a stringer, a live well or an ice box. An ice box, cooler or ice chest, is the best choice for keeping the fish in good condition, but most anglers use a stringer.

Under many conditions a stringer is adequate. It is not if you are fishing most of the day during hot weather, particularly if your fishing involves moving from one part of the lake to the other from time to time. To do that, of course, you must take the fish out of the water, and ten or fifteen minutes of exposure in hot weather is too much.

Most stringers will safely keep bass from escaping, but I dislike noisy ones. A metal stringer clanging against a metal boat is especially grating on my nerves, probably more so than it is on the bass. The plain rope stringers are silent, but on one of them the bass jam down on each other and won't live as long. If you get a prize bass and want to make sure you don't lose him, the rope stringer is ideal.

The best stringer I've found is one with plastic "snaps" on a nylon cord. Everything is quiet, and the individual holders slip up and down on the cord so that you can keep them in the boat until needed. To string one fish, it isn't necessary to lift the rest into the boat. The snaps have a locking device which makes them a bit unhandy to open, but this makes it virtually impossible for the bass to do it. The stringer is made by Sunset Line and Twine Company, Petaluma, California.

String bass through one lip or both? I have found no difference in how long they live regardless of which method is used, so I string them through the lower jaw. Stringing through both lips is supposed to keep the mouth shut, preventing the bass from drowning, but you shouldn't be dragging him that fast.

A live box is excellent for many occasions, but few boats have them built in on standard models. On small creeks this is the only practical method of keeping fish, since a stringer would be jerked off, and the boats are too small for most coolers.

The ice chest is my choice for most fishing trips, and what an improvement has been made in this item of equipment in the past decade. The light, inexpensive plastic foam boxes are excellent for keeping ice and fish, although they are not as durable as those with an outer covering of aluminum or hard plastic. When you buy a cooler for permanent use, get one with a lid you can open with one hand even when that hand is holding a bass. When you catch a bass, you want to be able to dispose of him quickly so you can get the lure back into the water at once.

Cleaning Your Catch

Always skin your bass. Nothing will add more to the good flavor of this fish. The "musky" taste which bass from some waters have, if cooked with the skin on, is absent once the skin is removed.

I fillet most of my bass, and recommend that you do the same. The methods shown in the drawings are the quickest and most effi-

HOW TO FILLET A BASS—METHOD #1

1. Start with head of fish pointing to your left (if you're right-handed).

2. Make first cut just behind the gill, stopping when the knife hits the backbone.

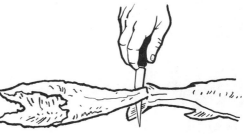

3. Without removing the knife, change direction of cut and slice down along the backbone, taking care not to cut through it.

4. Continue cut almost to tail, then turn fillet over. Angle knife through the meat to the skin, taking care not to cut through the skin.

5. By holding the knife almost parallel to your working surface, and using a sawing motion, you can separate meat from skin cleanly. Hold the tail end of the skin with left hand, partially pulling the fillet through the knife.

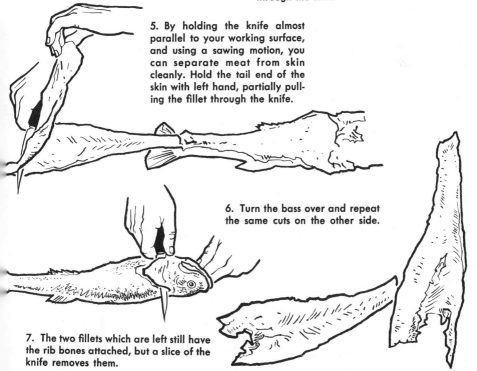

6. Turn the bass over and repeat the same cuts on the other side.

7. The two fillets which are left still have the rib bones attached, but a slice of the knife removes them.

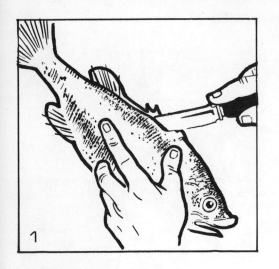

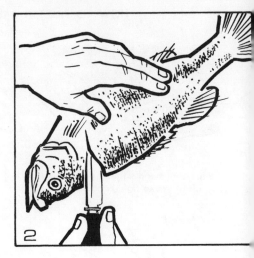

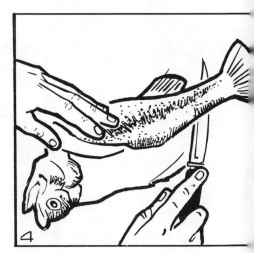

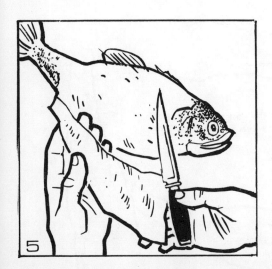

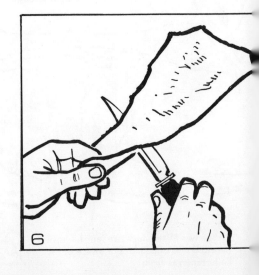

With a sharp knife, make a deep cut along one side of the dorsal fin from head to tail (1). Cut down to the ribs, and as you get behind the rib cage, slip the knife through the fish, staying close to the backbone to avoid waste. Turn the fish over and repeat the process on the other side. Now, beginning just behind the head, cut *around* the fish, close behind the gill covers, pectoral and pelvic fins (2). From this cut, slit the belly, joining the cuts where you came through from the back. Using your fingers and the point of the knife, carefully free the flesh from the rib bones on one side, then the other (3) and cut the fillet loose (4). To skin, remove the fillet (5) and start the skin separating from the flesh at the tail end. Grasp the skin and peel, using the knife flat to aid the process (6). *Courtesy Shakespeare Co.*

HOW TO SKIN A BASS WITHOUT FILLETING IT

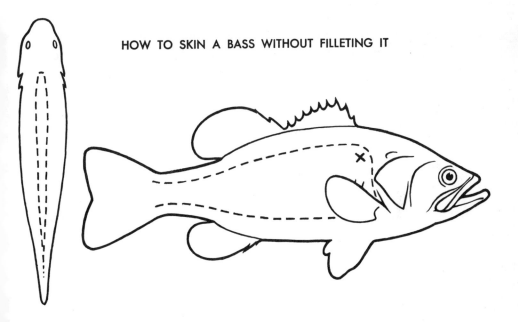

With a sharp knife, make shallow cuts through the skin as shown by the dotted lines in drawing at left. The cuts along each side of the backbone will join just behind the dorsal fin. Then grab the skin at point X (above), and peel the skin from that side with a steady pull. Repeat on the other side. To complete the cleaning process, strip out the backbone and dorsal fins by grasping the backbone with pliers just behind the dorsal fin and pulling. Finally, remove the head and belly waste by cutting along the dotted line from X clockwise to the tail.

cient I've ever found, and the easiest once you acquire the dexterity which comes with practice. There is little waste in meat left along the backbone but, if even that concerns you, chop that backbone portion out and cook it along with the fillets as an extra for those who like to pick around the bones.

A good fillet knife is vital to do this job properly. It should have a handle which is big enough to hold and which doesn't become slippery when wet. The blade should be at least 7 inches long along the flat edge, not counting the upsweep near the point, and it should be flexible but with enough backbone to slice through heavy bass ribs. An ordinary butcher knife, with a wooden handle and a long, narrow blade, fits these requirements.

Exceptionally big bass, say over 5 pounds, are rather difficult to fillet using the first method shown simply because the rib bones are exceedingly hard to cut. For them use the alternate fillet method. You may prefer it for all of your filleting.

If you consider a bass too small to fillet, yet still need it for the pot, follow the third set of diagrams. Use the same method on a big fish if you want it whole for baking.

Storing Fish

The quicker bass are eaten after being caught the better they are, and they are better if eaten fresh than if frozen and thawed later.

If you find it necessary to keep them for more than twenty-four hours after cleaning, which is usually the case, you should freeze them. Just how you accomplish this is important to how they will taste later.

If you must wrap them for freezing with either foil or freezer paper, use several layers and seal the package well with freezer tape to keep out as much air as possible. A far better method is to freeze them in water.

Wax-coated milk cartons are ideal containers to use for freezing fillets or small fish left whole. Use either the one-quart or the half-gallon size, depending upon how much fish you have. Put the fish in the carton, fill it to within an inch of the top with water, and place in the "quick freeze" portion of your freezer. Make sure you label the cartons as to contents, since it's impossible to tell what is in the ice just from looking. Stored in this manner, fish will keep for weeks and yet still have a flavor closely approaching that of the fresh variety.

How to Cook Bass

There are as many ways to cook fish as there are to catch them, and the diversity of taste among people insures that all methods have merit for some. Most common are frying, baking and broiling, but bass can also be poached, made into fish cakes, or used in a stew, courtbouillon or sauce piquante.

In the realm of gastronomical pleasures, fried bass fillets are in a class by themselves. Season the fillets with salt and pepper, and coat them with fresh, yellow corn meal which has also been seasoned with salt and pepper. Place the fillets in a bowl of cold water, and the seasoned corn meal in a paper bag. Salt and pepper each fillet and drop it in the bag, then shake up the whole batch at one time.

Fry the fish in an iron skillet, in deep fat. Get that fat smoking hot before you ease the fillets into it.

A good way to test your fat for the right heat is to float a kitchen match in it. When it ignites, start cooking. The grease or cooking oil will pop and sputter a bit when you add the fillets, so peace is best kept in the household if you do your cooking outside.

When you fill the skillet with fish this will cool the fat down a bit, but you will have accomplished the initial searing which is all important to have greaseless fried fish. Turn once, and remove when brown on both sides. Place the fillets on absorbent paper of some kind, such as paper towels or paper bags, so that any fat will drain.

By the time you get the first batch out of the pan, the fat will probably have again reached that smoking-hot point, ready for the next one. Manipulate the heat under the skillet to achieve the results you want, *but never, never let the fat get below the "hot" point.* If you do the inevitable result will be soggy fish.

If the fillets are thick, score them with a knife at intervals of about an inch, or chop the big ones in half so they are more manageable in the pan. For variety, try slicing the fillets into "fish sticks" before frying.

Hush Puppies and Stuff

There are as many recipes for hush puppies as for cooking fish, and they vary from excellent to awful. Here is my wife Mary's recipe, which is excellent:

2 cups sifted corn meal	½ teaspoon soda
½ cup flour	3 teaspoons baking
1 egg	powder
1 cup diced onions	2 teaspoons salt

buttermilk and beer (half and half)

Mix dry ingredients. Stir in beaten egg. Add onions to the batter. Mix with buttermilk and beer until thick. Drop batter, 1 tablespoon at a time, in deep fat in which fish has been fried.

I usually cook some of the hush puppies along with the fish, dropping them in between the fillets in odd corners of the skillet. In this case you should wait until the fat has cooled a bit, since the puppies cook more quickly than do the fillets and the smoking hot fat will burn them. When cooking nothing but hush puppies, after the fish are out of the pan, reduce the heat slightly. Keep them turning and don't overcook.

For an unusual flavor, chop a raw bass fillet up into very fine pieces—almost grated—and add to the hush puppy batter.

Drain the hush puppies on absorbent paper just as you do the fish, and cook twice as many as you think you'll need.

A fresh green salad of your choice, plus sliced onions and pickles, is all that is needed with fried bass fillets and hush puppies.

Broiled Bass Fillets

Salt and pepper the bass fillets well, then place them on aluminum foil under a moderately hot broiler. Brush them with melted butter into which you've squeezed half a lemon. Cook until the fillets are done to your taste halfway through, then turn them over.

At frequent intervals, brush the fillets again with the butter-lemon sauce or rub the hot fillets with the end of a stick of butter and squeeze a few drops of lemon juice on them.

When the fish are almost done to your taste, brush with butter once more and turn the broiler up very hot. Serve when the fillets

turn a golden brown on top, which will take only two or three
minutes under the hot fire.

Baked Bass

Marinate whole bass in salted milk (1 teaspoon per cup), brush
with melted butter, and sprinkle with sieved crumbs and paprika.
Place on a well-greased shallow pan and bake in moderately hot
oven (375° to 400°) until meat will flake away from bones easily.
Baste with melted butter at least twice during the cooking.

III

THE EQUIPMENT

CHAPTER TWENTY-THREE

Fly Fishing

Fᴌʏ fishing came first. Before anyone ever dreamed of such methods as plug casting, spinning or spincasting, anglers were taking fish on flies. It was with the fly rod that Henshall popularized fishing for the black bass, and fly fishing for bass remains one of the most satisfying forms of the sport. Other methods are more versatile, able to cope with the habits, habitats and moods of our fish under a greater range of conditions, but for many situations fly-rodding for bass can only be described as utterly deadly.

Fly casting is entirely different from the other forms of casting. The line itself is actually cast, with the lure just going along for the ride at the end of the leader. In all other forms of casting—plug, spinning or spincasting, the lure is cast and the line is pulled along with it.

A fly line, obviously, must be fairly heavy if it is to be cast any distance, and this is why fly lines are of larger diameter than casting or spinning lines. How big and how heavy depends upon the rod with which the line is used. Thus there are a variety of fly lines available to match various rods.

How to Fly Cast

Fly casting is not difficult. Anyone with a normal degree of coordination can acquire adequate bass-fishing proficiency within a fairly short time, provided he follows the instructions in this chapter—and PRACTICES. Fishing, for the beginner, is not practice. This is particularly true where fly casting is concerned. It is important that the novice learn the rudiments of this type of fishing unencumbered by hooks, trees . . . or fish.

Begin your fly-casting training, if possible, on a lawn. In addition to being free of trees and bushes, there will be fewer problems of pickup from the water which tend to give trouble to the beginner. The grass protects the fly line from damage.

In the crudest sense, fly casting consists of: 1) throwing the fly line into the air behind you; and 2) throwing it out front into the water.

To "throw" the line, of course, you use the fly rod. Now, let's break those two movements down into four, refining it a bit and applying more conventional terminology. There are only four parts of the normal fly cast: 1) pickup; 2) backcast; 3) pause; 4) forward cast. Failure to properly execute any one of these will insure poor results.

Pickup. Start with rod almost parallel to the water (grass), pointing down the line, and with both arms comfortably extended in front of you. Raise the rod slowly until the line is almost free of the lawn, with the end of it moving slowly toward you.

Backcast. Keeping your right wrist firm, apply power smartly to flip the line high into the air behind you. Stop the power of your backcast when the rod reaches the one or two o'clock position.

Pause. This means exactly what it says. Do nothing at this point except wait until the line straightens out behind you.

Forward Cast. Lower the right elbow slightly and push the rod forward, aiming at a point 10 or 15 feet above where you want the lure to land.

Follow those directions, and practice for one hour, and I promise you'll be getting out a fairly decent line.

Now for some finer points in those four steps.

The greatest mistakes of beginning fly casters, and of many, many experienced fishermen, are: 1) trying to pick up the line too suddenly, before most of it is lifted from the water by a raising of arm and rod; 2) taking the rod back too far on the backcast, either from taking the forearm back too far or from breaking the wrist; 3) failure to pause the proper length of time between backcast and forward cast; and 4) chopping downward on the forward cast rather than pushing the rod forward.

Most important: On your backcast aim at a point high *above* the water behind you; on the forward cast aim at a point 10 or 15 feet *above* the water out front.

Let your left hand, which plays an important part in handling the line, generally duplicate the path of the right hand throughout the cast. On the backcast it comes across the body and up, then precedes the right on the forward cast down and outward.

How long to pause between backcast and forward cast is not an exact thing. It is the time required for the line to roll over and straighten out behind, pulling the rod into action, but that time varies depending upon such factors as wind, length of line you have out, the characteristics of your rod and the way you cast. In the beginning just turn your head and *look* to see if the line has reached the proper point. With experience, you will soon be able to feel the tug on your rod and know when to drop that elbow and drive forward.

"Shooting line" means casting out a greater length of line forward than you have out on your backcast. Do it by having extra line pulled from the reel, coiled or looped in your left hand, and allowing it to be pulled out through the guides by the force of the forward cast. Instead of holding the loose line in your hand you can allow it to fall on the water (if you're wading) or in a clear spot in the boat.

Distance in fly casting is primarily a question of line and rod tip speed, which go together. After you have mastered the basic cast, you will learn to increase that line and rod speed by manipulating your left hand and arm. Pulling down on the line with your left hand accentuates the action of the rod, and by coordinating movements of your two arms you can increase the power of the cast.

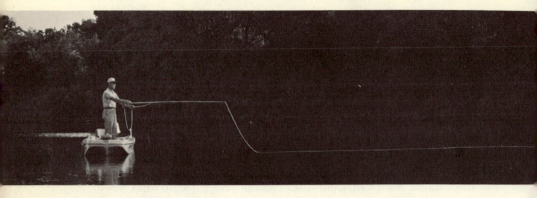

1. Begin cast with the rod horizontal and the line resting on the water. Arms should be extended; left hand holds the line just above the reel.

2. The Pickup. Raise rod slowly so the line comes smoothly off the water. Avoid whipping the line off the water too suddenly.

3. Beginning of Backcast (below). When all the line is clear of the water, apply power to the backcast and flip the line into the air behind you.

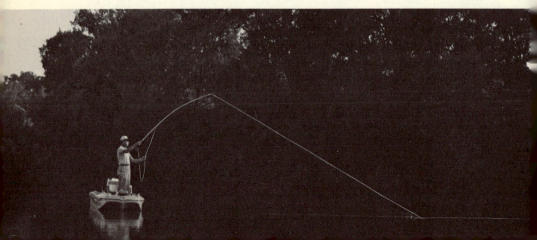

4. Near End of Backcast. Continue to apply power to about this point, then allow rod to coast back slightly beyond vertical position.

5. As line begins to straighten behind you, glance over your shoulder to watch it straighten completely. Eventually you will be able to *feel* it.

6. **Beginning of Forward Cast.** Left hand follows right hand back and then precedes it forward, pulling on line to give added action to rod.

7. **Forward Cast.** Dropping elbow slightly, apply full power at this point, aiming for a spot 10 or 15 feet above where you want lure to land.

8.   Forward Cast. Rather than chopping downward at the completion of forward cast, push rod forward and upward, keeping line above the water.

9.   Forward Cast. Line rolls out in a tight bow, forward thrust of rod diminishing. Left hand releases line, which shoots through guides.

The ultimate in the use of the line-hand pull is called the double-haul cast. It is rarely needed in practical bass fishing, but worth learning when you have progressed to the proper point.

The Fly Reel

In fly fishing for bass the reel is simply something to conveniently hold the line. It plays no part in either casting, retrieving or in playing a fish. That being the case, any reel you prefer will serve the purpose, whether it be a single action or an automatic. The latter is somewhat more convenient for retrieving loose line but can be irritating when you accidentally trip the trigger as you put the rod down. Take your choice.

On a moderately heavy rod, however, you should get a moderately heavy reel for proper balance. Casting with an outfit which

Do not break wrist on the backcast as this causes the line to drop too low behind you, often hitting the water.

1. Begin cast with the rod horizontal and a few feet of line coiled in the left hand.

2. As you begin the backcast, pull downward on the line held in the left hand.

3.   When the backcast is at its maximum point, let the left hand follow the right hand and release loose line, allowing line to feed into backcast.

4.   As forward cast begins, reach back with the left hand, grab the line as high as possible and pull down strongly.

5. Hold the line in the left hand until the thrust of the forward cast is greatest...

6. Then release line and let it shoot through the rod guides, giving added distance to the cast.

has the balance point too far forward puts quite a strain on the wrist.

The Fly Rod for Bass

The bass-fishing fly rod for the average angler should be of medium weight and medium action. It should be from 8 to 9 feet in length.

Bamboo has almost disappeared as a material for fly rods. The only significant exceptions are the very excellent, and expensive, resin-impregnated bamboo rods made by The Orvis Company of Manchester, Vermont.

These Orvis rods deserve special mention. The process by which the bamboo is impregnated makes it waterproof to the core, impervious to sun or humidity. They are meticulously handcrafted under the supervision of Wes Jordon, one of the greatest rod makers of all time. These Orvis rods are a delight to use.

Tubular steel was making some inroads upon bamboo as a fly-rod material shortly before World War II, but that synthetic substance called fiberglass revolutionized the industry. Glass rods are now overwhelmingly dominant in tackle stores and in the field. Earlier ones left much to be desired, but continued research has resulted in glass rods which leave nothing to be desired as a fishing tool. Most manufacturers now produce only glass rods, and even the very moderately priced ones are amazingly efficient.

Avoid rods with a very fast, light tip and also those with a buggy whip, "wet rag" action. The fly rod for bass must have muscle because of the big, wind-resistant bass bugs and the heavy spinner-streamers which will be used many times.

Select the fly line recommended by the rod manufacturer. This may not result in exactly the combination you'll want later, for individual tastes vary and the right line for a rod isn't limited to one exact weight, but the one called for in the maker's specifications will be fully satisfactory.

Advantages and Disadvantages

Most fishermen get a greater thrill from fighting a bass on a fly rod than they do using any of the shorter rods. The angler feels the resistance of the fish more, simply because the bass can apply greater leverage through the long wand.

The fly rod enables us to use smaller, lighter lures than we can use with other methods. With it we can also drift those flies and bass bugs down to the surface of lake or stream with scarcely a ripple. With a fly rod, in other words, lures can be presented to the fish more delicately than in any other manner.

Another advantage of the long rod is that we can apply more power and leverage with it in playing a fish than with any of the shorter sticks. It is a killing weapon.

Delicate but deadly is an apt description of a well-balanced, expertly crafted fly rod, and this is undoubtedly one reason why fly fishing has been a kingly sport for centuries.

As for the disadvantages, the greatest for bass fishermen is that it is difficult—often impossible—to fly fish a lure down deep where bass spend much of their time. Even with the new fast-sinking fly lines, it is impractical to work lures at depths which can be effectively reached with other methods. Fly fishing obviously limits the size and actions of the lures which can be used.

Last, and seldom important except in specialized situations, the length of a fly rod makes it impossible to use in thickly vegetated areas.

Strike and Fight

Peculiar to fly fishing is the fact that your rod should be pointed toward your lure much of the time while you're fishing. The reason is that this position gives you quicker striking response once the bass hits.

On any rod the tip momentarily goes *forward* when you heave *backward* on the handle to set the hook. With a fly rod this movement in the wrong direction is accentuated and prolonged by the length of the rod. Pointing the rod toward the lure during the retrieve eliminates some of this lag.

Fishing underwater lures, wet flies or spinner-fly combinations, you can retrieve either by gathering the line in your left hand or by stripping the line in with that left hand. Try both until you discover which the bass prefer that particular day.

Another favorite method of fishing a spinner-streamer or spinner-hackle combination, one which I probably use more than either of the above, doesn't involve any retrieving of line. I end my cast with the fly rod low over the water, pointing directly at the lure, then retrieve the lure several feet by slowly raising the rod tip. When the rod is in proper position for a pickup for the next cast, I make that next cast.

Dry flies are effective on bass as they are on trout, at times, but when I go to the surface I invariably turn to bass bugs. Fly rodding for bass with these lures is one of the most pleasant ways for an angler to spend a lifetime or two, and it is terribly effective if the fish are in range of surface lures.

Bass will reject an artificial bug quickly, which demands meticulous attention to your lure and immediate striking in order to set the hook. Bass bugs are worked by little twitches and jerks of the rod, and here you must take care not to let that rod approach the vertical while working the lure. Too much sag in the line is the result, and added to the aforementioned lag of the long rod, it makes setting the hook almost impossible.

Use your left hand as well as your right when setting the hook with a fly rod. Strip line with it as you simultaneously raise your rod and action will be transmitted to the hook more quickly.

When the bass is hooked, play the fish with the rod at about a 45-angle by stripping in line. Remember—the reel isn't used to play the fish in fly-rod fishing. Some species of fish which make long runs, particularly the saltwater varieties, are played from the reel, and in this case a single-action reel is mandatory, but I've never encountered a bass which couldn't be handled with the spring of the fly rod plus giving a little line with the left hand. I live in hope of finding one.

Plug Casting

Plug casting is a purely American invention. It was made possible by the invention of the multiplying casting reel in about 1810 by George Snyder, a watchmaker and silversmith of Paris, Kentucky. How well Snyder designed that first reel is evidenced by the fact that modern casting reels, a century and a half later, are virtual copies of those early models. There have been many refinements, of course, with the past two decades producing a number of significant improvements resulting from better materials and techniques of manufacture.

Plug casting is probably the most difficult form of casting to master, because it involves educating the thumb through long practice. It is also, for those who are adept, the most accurate method of all.

The principle of this form of casting is that the lure pulls line from the reel, causing the spool on which the line is wound to revolve. The spool must start to revolve suddenly at the beginning of the cast, must pay out line in ratio to the pull of the lure as it travels through the air and must be made to cease revolving as soon as the lure touches the water. If the last is not accomplished, a tangle of line which we call a backlash, is the result.

The angler's thumb is the mechanism which controls these actions. It holds the spool firmly during the backcast, releases it at the proper point on the forward cast, delicately varies pressure on the line throughout the cast, and stops the spool when the lure touches the water.

Plug-Casting Rods

Plug-casting rods range from 7 feet in length on downward. For most, and especially for the beginner, the length should be from 5 to 6 feet. The action should extend well down into the rod, as opposed to the fast-tip design which starts the spool with a jerk that is difficult to control.

The longer the rod and the lighter the action, the smaller the lures that can be comfortably handled. The ¼ ounce lures are the lightest practical weight for plug casting, but the method is at its best with those ranging from ⅜ ounce to ¾ ounce matched with a medium-action rod 5½ or 6 feet long.

As with all fishing equipment, get the best casting rod you can afford. Very good ones are moderately priced. The tip guide is extremely important, since a soft one will be scored by the line and will continually weaken the line. Good ones of carboloy or other extremely hard alloys save their cost in lures not lost, not to mention fish. Agate guides are good but are more fragile. The difference between the most expensive and moderate-priced rods is in the fittings. The rod blanks are often the same, but the top rods have better guides, ferrules and handles.

Plug-Casting Reels

As contrasted with fly casting, the reel used in plug casting is extremely important. The modern reel is much the same as the one invented by Snyder, but the performance differs widely. The moderately priced plug-casting reels available now in the $10 to $15 range are superior to most of the very expensive casting reels available before World War II.

Free-spool reels are becoming more popular with many anglers, with the Garcia Ambassadeur, made in Sweden, leading the way.

With these reels, the spool revolves during the cast but the handles and/or the gears of the reel do not.

Most reels have brakes to prevent or minimize backlashes. If they are used properly all are effective to a degree, and the beginner will find them helpful until his thumb becomes fully educated. As rapidly as possible, however, he should gradually eliminate the use of the brake, for all of them decrease the efficiency of the reel.

How To Plug Cast

Begin your cast by pointing your rod, raised at an angle of about 45 degrees, toward the target. Many tournament casters use the first guide of the rod as a sight, which gives you an idea what the initial rod position should be.

The reel handles should be UP at the start of the cast (assuming you are right-handed), for three very important reasons: 1. The reel itself is more efficient in that position. 2. Your wrist works freely in this position during the cast. 3. Only in this position can your thumb provide the delicate braking action on the spool which is vital to successful casting.

In plug casting there are only two steps: backcast and forward cast. The pickup of the fly cast is eliminated, because the lure is from 2 to 6 inches from the rod tip when the cast is begun. The pause between the backcast and the forward cast of the fly fisherman is fatal to plug casting.

Bring the rod straight back in a vertical plane, with your thumb firmly on the reel spool, and stop it at a point somewhere between 1 and 2 o'clock. Using the same forearm and wrist movement, and with *no* pause, apply power for the forward cast. Stop it at about a 10 o'clock position, releasing thumb pressure from the spool at about the same time. The lure will shoot out toward the target and you must reapply thumb pressure to slow the spool as the lure slows down.

It is extremely important, when learning to plug cast, to limit your early efforts to short casts. Use just enough force to get the lure to that nearby target in a gentle arc. Don't try to rifle the lure out on a plane parallel to the water, a difficult feat for the expert with this method.

1. Correct grip for plug casting (above), reel handles up, thumb on spool, and wrong grip (right).

2. Begin cast by pointing rod, raised at an angle of 45 degrees, toward the target. Some casters use the first guide of the rod as a sight.

3. Bring rod straight back, with thumb on reel spool, stopping between 1 and 2 o'clock, but do not pause as in fly casting. Begin forward cast immediately. If rod is kept vertical, lure will be propelled straight toward the target.

4. Bring rod forward, using forearm and wrist snap for power, and raise thumb from the spool. Follow through with the whole arm. When the lure nears the target, exert thumb pressure to slow the revolving spool.

The three-quarter cast, with the rod traveling midway between the vertical and horizontal positions, is comfortable and useful once an angler perfects the vertical cast and learns to control spool with thumb.

Switch hands for the retrieve while the lure is still in the air and start the lure toward you by sweeping back with the rod. While rod is still moving backward, begin the retrieve using the reel handles.

Maintain a firm grip on the rod during the retrieve by palming reel.

In plug casting, spinning and spincasting, the rod should be held at right angles to the line of retrieve (top left) or pointed slightly toward the lure (bottom left), but never away from the lure (above).

Greatest accuracy in all forms of casting stems from the vertical cast, since this virtually eliminates the direction problem. Despite this, you will find many occasions while fishing to deviate, to use a three-quarter or even a sidearm cast. Particularly in the case of plug casting, however, the beginner should learn the overhead cast, for any other is frequently dangerous to fishing companions.

Let me emphasize again the importance of having the reel handles up at beginning and end of the cast. If you have your thumb on top and try to make a vertical cast, that thumb must provide leverage for the cast and cannot possibly be as sensitive to decreasing spool diameter as the line pays out. In that position your wrist is locked, making effective use of it during the cast impossible.

Keep your casting reel *filled* with line. Failure to do so is one of the biggest mistakes of plug casters. The additional line isn't needed, but a full spool doesn't have to revolve as many times or as fast to lay out a certain length of line.

Advantages and Disadvantages

Plug casting is the most accurate of all casting methods. Lure retrieve is more positive and can be done more smoothly and more rapidly by the average angler. It is the ultimate method for manipulating large topwater bass plugs.

On the minus side, plug casting is difficult to learn, and is not as efficient at casting lures into the wind as are spinning and spincasting.

Key Points to Remember

Avoid fast-tip rod actions.
Avoid rods less than 5 feet long.
Begin cast with reel handles up.
Keep reel filled with line.
Practice.

CHAPTER TWENTY-FIVE

Spinning

Spinning began in Europe shortly before World War II, gradually infiltrated this country, and finally surged to popularity here in the decade from 1945 to 1955. It has been described as a halfway house between fly fishing and plug casting and it is, but it is much more, for spinning has virtues which are lacking in either fly fishing or plug casting. Spinning, in short, is a separate, distinct method of fishing, without a knowledge of which no angler can consider himself complete.

In fly casting the line is cast. In plug casting the line pays out from a revolving spool. In spinning the line spills from the end of a stationary spool.

Spinning rods are generally between casting and fly rods in length, running from 6½ to 7½ feet, but some of the ultra-light ones are only about 5 feet long. The spinning reel is mounted on this rod *below* the handle like the fly reel rather than above like the casting reel.

How to Cast

In spinning, a right-hander casts with the right hand and cranks in the retrieve with the left, for the reel handle on most spinning

1.   Holding rod with the reel foot between the second and third fingers, open the bail and pick up line with cushion of index finger (above). Do not hold line at the first joint of the finger (below).

2. Ready to cast. With rod raised at an angle of 45 degrees, sight along rod at the target.

3. Bring rod back smartly, stopping at 12 or 1 o'clock position.

4. Without pausing, flip the rod forward to the 9 or 10 o'clock position, extending index finger and releasing line just before rod's forward motion stops.

5. Point rod toward target and follow through as lure flies through air.

reels is mounted on the left. Some are available with right-hand crank for those who prefer it. Whereas in plug casting the line is controlled with the thumb, in spinning it is controlled with the first finger of the casting hand.

To assume the correct position for casting, reel in the lure until it is a few inches from the rod tip and the line feeding onto the reel is on top of it, nearest your hand. Reach down with your line finger (first finger of your casting hand) and pick up the line, holding it while you release the pickup device, or bail.

Now you're ready to cast. The procedure is almost identical to plug casting, although this time the reel is below the rod. Aim at your target through the first guide of the rod, with rod at about a 45-degree angle. Bring the rod back smartly but stop it at a 12 or 1 o'clock position. Flip forward, without pause, and continue the forward cast to about the 9 or 10 o'clock position, releasing the line slightly before the forward motion of the rod ceases.

The line is released simply by straightening out your finger. Some anglers think of it as pointing that line finger at the target. With a little practice you'll find that it is sufficiently positive to hold the line about midway between the tip of the finger and the first joint, although that will feel a bit insecure at first.

Notice that I referred to the forward cast as a "flip." For most anglers this is true, and here is where the fast-tip rod actions come into their own. With spinning you can *rifle* the lure toward the target virtually at eye level, since there is no problem of the spool starting, stopping or overrunning.

Begin your spinning practice by working toward a flat arc for your casts. You'll find this more pleasant and more satisfactory in a vast majority of fishing conditions, and you can master the other casting techniques as you progress.

You'll find that in spinning it isn't necessary to bring the rod back as far on the backcast as is true with plug casting, and in spinning you can release the line on the forward cast later. At the end of the cast you can just allow the lure to hit the water, since there will be no backlash, or you can stop the lure by one of two methods. The first is to make a forward turn on the reel handle, which engages the pickup and stops the line abruptly. A more delicate method is to feather the line with the same forefinger which released it.

Spinning Tackle

Spinning rods and reels come in a full range of sizes, from the ultra-light jobs to those suited for big-game angling. As is most often the case, the beginner is better off if he confines his first gear to the moderate range. Avoid the extremes in reel sizes, and get a 6½- or 7-foot rod, in a light to medium weight, with fast-tip action. Such a rig will superbly handle lure weights from ¼ ounce to ½ ounce, and do a passable job with those down to ⅛ ounce and up to ⅝.

Spinning rods aren't vastly different from long plug-casting rods, except that the reel seat is in a different location, but the spinning reel is unique. In all forms it is characterized by a spool which is stationary during the cast, and which moves forward and backward during the retrieve so that line wound on it by the pickup is distributed evenly.

But there the similarity between makes and models ends. Pickup devices come in a wide assortment of styles. There are full bails, half bails, manual pickups and automatic pickup arms. All have good points and bad points, and a choice here is a matter of personal preference. Let a good tackle salesman demonstrate all of them for you, then make your selection.

All spinning reels have drags which permit the fish to gain line if the pull exceeds a certain setting. This is a safety device which has saved countless fish for spin fishermen, since it compensates for an enormous number of angler errors.

The drag mechanisms on many early spinning reels were terrible. They were often erratic and jerky, and would not maintain a constant setting. Most of the very bad ones have fallen by the wayside, and even random reel selection now will probably result in a good drag for you.

When you set that drag, and the settting should be just below the breaking strength of the line, remember to set it while the line is through the rod guides in fishing position, tied to a door handle or something similar. If you test the drag simply by stripping line directly from the reel with your hand, you're guessing.

Unless used properly, the spinning reel is an invitation to twisted line. This is true because the pickup or bail puts twist in the line during each revolution it makes around the spool. That twist unwinds during each cast.

Trouble arises quite often when a new line is first wound onto the spool. If there are manufacturer's directions on the line which tell you how to put it on a spinning reel, follow them. If not, watch the line closely as you wind it on and use common sense. Check it now and then and, if twisting is apparent, try something else.

The simplest method is to put the spool of new line on the floor and stand over it with the reel. Let the line spill over the side of the spool (spool is stationary just as is the spool of the spinning reel), and make sure it is uncoiling in the same direction as the reel's pickup turns. If you get it wrong, severe twisting will be apparent in a few turns, in which case just turn the spool of new line over and let the line uncoil from the other side.

Another source of twisting in the line is reeling while the drag is slipping. If the drag is slipping, don't turn the crank.

Remember to play your fish by pumping the rod. Raise it up toward vertical slowly, then drop it swiftly back toward the water while you reel rapidly to gain line.

Advantages and Disadvantages

First, with spinning gear it is infinitely easier to cast than with either a fly rod or with a plug-casting outfit. The problem of timing inherent in fly fishing, and the delicate thumb control necessary to plug casting, are eliminated. Casting into the wind becomes possible for many for the first time. This one point, the ease of doing it, is one of its primary attractions.

Second, very light lures approaching fly-rod weight can be used in situations which eliminate the fly rod from consideration. They can be cast a greater distance than is possible for most people with the fly rod. The ease with which a lure can be flipped with a spinning rod makes it possible to use this rig in very restricted quarters. The bow and arrow cast, which is a gimmick when done with plug casting outfit, since it is beyond the skill of all but a few, became a legitimate tool when spinning arrived. With it any angler can learn to flip a lure 15 to 20 feet without making any cast at all.

Third, the drag mechanism on spinning reels brought a new efficiency to playing bass, particularly big bass. An ordinary angler from the standpoint of skill will now frequently land a lunker bass because of this new aid.

On the minus side, many fishermen don't like the character of spinning. They find the big reel hanging down below the rod awkward.

Spinning cannot handle true fly-rod lures with the efficiency of a fly rod, nor can it handle the very heavy lines and heavy lures with the efficiency possible in plug casting. It is not as accurate, for the skilled angler, as is plug casting.

Key Points to Remember

Keep your reel filled with line, but not overfilled. This is important. A half-filled spool *will not* cast efficiently. If it is overfilled, line will tend to spill and tangle.

Don't use a line heavier than that recommended for your reel.

Don't crank while the drag is slipping.

Pump your fish instead of "winching" it in.

CHAPTER TWENTY-SIX

Spincasting

SPINCASTING is a purely American invention which stemmed from satisfaction with the ease of spinning, but dissatisfaction with the method of line control and the unorthodox position of the reel on the rod. The spincast reel solved those problems.

This reel is essentially a spinning reel which has been enclosed with a cover, on which a push button has been mounted to control the line flow, and which is mounted on top of the rod like a plug-casting reel. For obvious reasons the spincast reel is often called the closed-face spinning reel or the push-button reel. Regardless of what it is called by anglers, tackle manufacturers call it a bonanza, as its development started countless new fishermen on their way to lake and stream.

Mr. Lloyd E. Johnson, a tool and die maker in Mankato, Minnesota, began development of the spincast reel shortly after the end of World War II. He was an ardent fisherman and wasn't satisfied with what was available, which was reason enough to make something better. In 1949, Johnson and H. Warren Denison, a fishing friend, set up their first factory in the basement of Johnson's home, and the Denison-Johnson Company began a new era in fishing.

Over the years Johnson received patents for many of his reel

1. Correct grip: handles up and thumb on push button.

2. Ready to cast: sight along rod at the target.

3. Mid-point of forward cast, rod tip doing most of the work. As rod comes forward, raise thumb from push button and release line.

4. End of cast: follow through as lure heads for target.

As in plug casting, palming reel is the best way to maintain a firm grip while retrieving the lure (top). Young anglers with small hands should use alternate grip (below). Rod can also be held in front of the reel.

designs, and has licensed other manufacturers to use some of them. One of the most important was the direct-drive principle with the power-shift handle. The direct-drive principle gave positive retrieve, overcoming the drag, but the power-shift handle permitted the drag to come into play when the handle was released. This gives the angler direct control of a fish when he wants it, but permits instant operation of the braking safety mechanism when desirable.

Spincasting is extremely easy. Anybody can learn it in minutes, and learn it well enough to catch fish. My children could spincast before they were big enough to hold the rod with one hand, and they were not precocious by any means.

As with plug casting and spinning, spincasting consists of two steps: backcast and forward cast. Assume the same position as when plug casting, with the reel handle pointing up. Press down on the push button with your thumb and hold it firmly. The casting movements are identical to those of spinning, but you release the line at the proper point of the forward cast by releasing the button instead of by letting the line slip off your forefinger.

Early spincast reels gave push-button control, freedom from backlashes, familiar rod and reel position, and ease of casting, but they left much to be desired in fishing efficiency. They were plagued with line twisting problems. Retrieve power was virtually absent. Line pickup was erratic. Drags were terrible. In the better spincast reels of today, however, most of these faults have been eliminated.

As with spinning, watch for line twist with the spincast reel. Make sure the new line is put on properly, and don't reel while the drag is slipping (impossible on direct drive reels since the drag is inoperative while the handle is being turned).

There is one reel design which does not add twist if you reel while the drag is slipping. The pickup arm backs up as the fish takes out line, which unwinds line from the spool. Most spools revolve as the drag slips, which does cause twist, but this is not fatal unless you accentuate the situation by reeling vigorously at the same time.

Spincast reels are also made for mounting beneath the rod in spinning position. In these the line is held against the underside of the rod with the forefinger during the casting operation. Another recent design is a further move toward integrating the two methods of casting. It is a spinning reel mounted beneath the rod, but which is controlled by a push button built into the top of the rod.

Any rod which can be used for plug casting can be used for spincasting. Many manufacturers, in fact, label their rods as adaptable to either method. Fast-tip actions are fine for spincasting. The beginning spincaster should get a rod measuring from 5½ to 6½ feet in length, light to medium weight, with a progressive taper.

Key Points to Remember

Keep your reel filled with line, but not overfilled. This is important. A half-filled spool *will not* cast efficiently, and greatly decreases drag efficiency and retrieve power.

Don't use a line heavier than that recommended for the reel.

Don't crank while the drag is slipping.

Pump your fish instead of "winching" it in.

CHAPTER TWENTY-SEVEN

Lines, Leaders and Knots

Fly Lines

Fʟʏ lines are manufactured today exclusively of braided nylon or dacron, and here is just about the only place where dacron enters the picture for bass fishermen. These lines are superior to the old ones of silk in every respect. They float when they should float and sink when they should sink. They have a hard, slick finish which resists abrasion and slides through rod guides with ease. Most fly lines are made of braided nylon but a few sinking lines are of braided dacron.

For reasons already discussed, the fly line is of utmost importance in fly fishing. In order to enjoy maximum performance from a particular rod, that line must be matched to the rod.

Before the introduction of nylon and dacron, fly lines had a letter designation which denoted the diameter of the line. Since all silk lines were of about the same consistency, this system adequately indicated the weight of the line as well. When nylon and dacron came in the old designations lost meaning, since weight-diameter ratios varied widely. Confusion was the order of the day.

To bring some order out of the chaos, the American Fishing Tackle Manufacturers Association (AFTMA) devised a new fly-line standard of number designations, and all fly lines are so marked now. It is based on the weight in grains of the first 30 feet of the line, exclusive of any taper tip.

Preceding the number designation of the fly line in this new system is a letter symbol telling what kind of line it is: L-Level; DT—Double Taper; WF—Weight Forward. Following the number designation is another letter indicating whether the line floats or sinks: F—Floating; S—Sinking. A level floating line which would have been a "D" under the old system, is now an "L7F."

For most fly-rod bass fishing a floating line is best. Even with it, underwater lures can be worked 5 or 6 feet down since the leader will sink. If you insist on using a fly rod to bass fish deeper than that, and it can be done although I don't find it satisfactory, get a sinking fly line. Don't try to use it with surface bugs, however.

A level fly line is the same diameter throughout its length. It is the least expensive of all, and is perfectly satisfactory for bass fishing.

The weight forward (WF—variously called rocket taper, bug taper and torpedo head) fly line has a short, tapered forward section of about 10 feet; then a short, heavy, level section of about 14 feet; and finally a long remaining section of light, level line. It is ideal for shooting line, for making long casts. It is expensive compared to the level line, usually costing three to five times as much, and I would not recommend it for the beginning bass fisherman.

The WF line will handle big, wind-resistant bass bugs considerably better than will a level line, but it is only with medium to long casts that this becomes an appreciable advantage. On short casts, in fact, I find the level line more pleasant to use, because the heavy shooting portion of the line frequently pulls the light forward portion backward through the guides when you pause in your fishing and raise the rod tip. For making medium to long casts, however, particularly into any breeze, the WF line is excellent.

The double-taper (DT) line is just what the name implies. It has a long, level center section, and is tapered at both ends. When one end is worn or damaged, the line can be reversed on the reel. I see little need for a DT line in bass fishing. It is somewhat superior to the level line in handling dry flies, but this is not the forte of bass fishermen.

Silk lines required constant care in order to keep them floating. It was necessary to apply line dressing at frequent intervals during the day's fishing, and one of the great topics of discussion among fly fishermen centered around which line dressing was best.

Modern floating lines of braided nylon, made to float by a variety of manufacturing methods, are tremendous improvements, but they do need some attention. They should be kept clean! Scum from the water will cause a line to sink, and should be removed with the line cleaner which comes with many lines, or with soap and clean water.

Protect the finish of your fly line. Avoid dragging it over rough logs, rocks or boat edges.

It isn't necessary to remove a fly line from the reel at night, but it is advisable to do so if it's not to be used for some months. Just wind it in big, loose coils and hang it up. If it remains on the reel, unused for long periods, it tends to take a "set" in those tight coils.

Lines for Casting, Spinning and Spincasting

The braided nylon lines used for spinning and casting can be either a soft braid or a hard braid. The former behaves better on the reel, casts better, but is less waterproof and less durable.

Braided line is excellent for plug-casting reels, has considerable advantage at times with spinning, but should not be used on spincasting reels. It is especially desirable for plug casting, where line control on the revolving spool is critical, since it "lays on" the spool much better than does monofilament. The latter tends to balloon out from the spool during a cast under less experienced thumbs.

This same trait of behaving better on the reel makes braided line pleasant to use on spinning reels, although far more anglers use monofilament in this instance.

Braided line floats whereas monofilament sinks. If you're fishing surface lures braided is best, since it gives better control of the lure. The weight of a sinking monofilament line will move a floating plug, which often isn't desirable.

For fishing deep-running lures, particularly bottom bumpers, monofilament has a decided advantage because it does sink.

Braided lines costs more but lasts longer. With it use a monofilament leader, which is more resistant to abrasion from the rod-tip guide during the cast, and is less apt to spook bass in very clear water.

Monofilaments available today are infinitely superior to the best ones on the market a decade ago. The old ones were wiry and stiff, and rapidly became more so with exposure to light and sun. Many were so elastic that it was difficult to set the hook.

Now you can buy monofilaments which are very limp, non-elastic and resistant to deterioration. Knot strength on the better new lines is good, something else which was missing in earlier ones.

Poor monofilament is still available, so beware of bargains. Most of the major tackle companies have good mono, so it pays to stick with reputable names. Excellent ones in the field right now are Dupont's Stren, Gladding's Gladyl, Cortland's 7-Star, Garcia's Platyl, Berkley's Trilene and Shakespeare's 7000. There are other good ones, but all may be obsolete before this book is in print very long. The search for new and better ways to catch more fish, through chemistry, goes on and on.

I doubt that the color of a line makes any difference in its fish-catching potential. The fluorescent monofilament, however, does make it easier for the angler to follow the course of his own line.

The weight of the line you use should be determined by your rod and reel, the lures you are fishing, and the conditions under which you are fishing. Don't use a line heavier than that recommended by the manufacturer of your reel, in the case of spinning or spincasting. In all cases, *the lighter the line the easier it is to cast, and the easier it is to cast light lures.* Fishing light jigs down deep where feel is extremely important requires a light line. You need to know precisely when a bass takes the lure in his mouth, and this is best accomplished with light spinning or spincasting gear and light line—6-pound test, for instance.

For average bass fishing, the heaviest line which can pleasantly be used *should* be used. You'll lose fewer lures; you'll lose less time getting "hung up," since you can jerk your lure loose most of the time; and you'll certainly land more bass, especially big ones.

Many spincasting reels will not cast well with line of over 8-pound test. If that's the case, use it. Others do well with 15- or 20-pound line.

On open-faced spinning reels, heavy-test monofilament line tends to spill and tangle if it isn't extremely limp, so use care that you don't go too heavy for efficient operation of the equipment. On my spinning rigs I seldom go below 8-pound test and rarely over 12.

Plug-casting reels will effectively handle much heavier lines than can regular-sized spinning or spincasting rigs. With them there is little point in going below 10-pound line, and if you like you can go on up to 20- or 25-pound test. I use 15-, 17-, or 20-pound test most of the time. At least half of the bass-fishing experts of my acquaintance, throughout the nation, use 20 pound.

A fishing line is subject to an enormous amount of abuse which renders the breaking strength far less than that listed on the box. Knots chop it down. Flexing from a vibrating lure weakens it. Friction from the tip guide during casting weakens it. Worn guides weaken it. Rocks and stumps and lure hooks weaken it. The heavier the line you use, the more insurance you're buying against this attrition.

Many of the best bass lakes in the nation are literally loaded with bass cover–trees, stumps, limbs, logs, weed beds and the like. When a 6- or 8-pound bass takes a half-hitch around a stump with your 8-pound line and gets a running start, the results are predictable. If it's a 20-pound line there is room for doubt.

With very light line you've got to take too long to play a good bass down. You must work him with care until he's ready for thumb or net, and during that time it's quite possible that you could have landed two other fish. I can't emphasize too strongly that, once you hook a bass, you should get him in the boat in short order and get your lure working again.

Leaders

For bass bugging with a fly rod, use a monofilament nylon leader of about 10-pound test and about 6 or 8 feet long. Just a length of level mono line will do fine under most conditions.

For better performance with wind-resistant bugs, particularly under windy conditions, use a tapered leader. Keep the tip test out where the bug is tied at around 10-pound test, but graduate the leader back toward the line to about 25- or 30-pound test. You can make these by joining monos of various weights, or you can buy knotless tapered leaders.

When using braided line on spinning or casting gear, always

use a monofilament leader. Mono resists the abrasion which occurs near the lure during casting, and is less visible to fish.

A shock leader of heavier test mono is frequently desirable whether braided or monofilament line is being used. It takes the wear near the lure, and gives extra strength out at the tip where a bass often breaks the line by fouling it on underwater obstructions. This shock leader can be just a heavier length of level mono, or it can be a knotless tapered leader used in reverse fashion. One of my favorites is a 7-foot leader which tests 8 pounds at the butt and 25 pounds at the tip, and I use it with 8- or 10-pound line. Another is a 15-foot leader which is 18 pounds at the butt and 50 at the tip, which I match with 15- or 20-pound-test line. With this latter, however, I usually cut 3 or 4 feet from the tip, which gives a more manageable diameter yet one which still tests about 40 pounds.

Knots

At no other skill are reasonably good bass fishermen so inept as in tying a good knot for the purpose at hand. The skill is vital since a poor knot can decrease your effective line strength as much as 50 percent.

In theory the best knots sometime will test 100 percent of the rated strength of the line. In practice all knots cut your line strength somewhat. The object, therefore, is to use the best knot for a particular purpose and to tie it as best you can each time. The latter is important, for a poorly tied knot loses much of its effectiveness.

Select the knots you like—three or four will cover just about any contingency in bass fishing—and learn them well. Learn them by practicing, just as you would with any other skill, and do it at home.

For attaching *leader to fly line*, the Nail Knot or Tube Knot is strongest and neatest. The metal eyelet which is inserted in the end of the fly line to attach a leader works well with level lines. When using a tapered fly line it is difficult to get this eyelet into the line; therefore, use the Nail Knot or the Tube Knot.

For joining *monofilament nylon to monofilament*, use the Blood Knot if the line diameters are similar, or the Surgeon's Knot if the lines are of unequal diameter.

For joining *braided nylon to monofilament*, use either the Key's Knot or the Surgeon's Knot.

For tying *monofilament to a lure or hook eye*, use the Improved Clinch Knot.

Decide which knots you prefer to use for the situations you encounter, learn them well, and stick with them.

An Overhand Knot is the kind of knot you tie in your shoe lace just before you tie the bow. Get it firmly in mind that this is one knot you do *not* want to use in fishing. It's sometimes called the Wind Knot because you'll frequently tie one in your leader while you're casting, particularly if fly fishing. Watch for it, since it will cut your effective line strength by as much as one half.

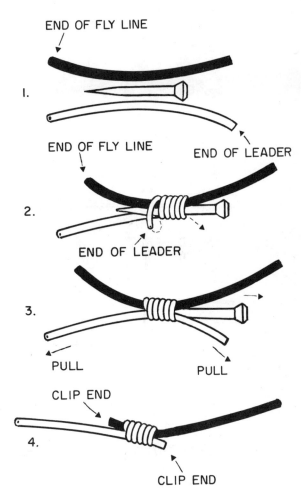

The Nail Knot is used to tie the butt end of the leader to the end of the fly line in order to make a smooth join that will slide through the rod guides. A tapered nail is used in tying this knot. To tie the knot, lay the line and leader parallel to each other, with the nail between (1). Wind leader downward around the nail, line and itself six times; then run end of leader back through the loops (2). Pull both ends of leader tight and slip the knot down the nail, tightening it as you do so (3). Slip the nail out and re-tighten the knot by pulling leader ends. Pull the line and leader tight and clip ends close to knot (4).

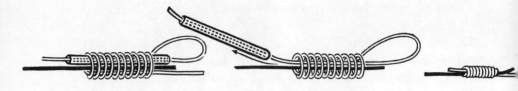

The Tube Knot is tied exactly like the Nail Knot except that a small tube is used instead of a nail. The leader is pushed *through* the tube and the tube is then slipped out and the knot tightened.

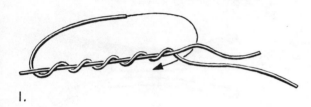

1.

2.   HOLD HERE

3.

The Blood Knot is used for tying monofilament of the same diameter. To tie the knot, lay the two strands parallel to each other and twist one around the other (1), making at least five turns. Then place the end between the strands, as shown by the arrow. Hold the end at point X and wind the other short end around the main strand the same number of turns, but in the opposite direction (2). The knot would look as in 3 if held firmly in place; actually, as soon as released the turns equalize. Pulling on both ends of the monofilament tightens the knot (4). Clip off ends and it is finished.

4

The Surgeon's Knot is also used for tying two strands of monofilament. It can be used to tie a tippet to a tapered leader. Lay the ends to be joined parallel to each other with an ample overlap. Tie a simple overhand knot, pulling the free end all the way through; then tie another one. Pull tight and clip the ends.

The Key's Knot is used for tying monofilament leader to braided casting line. Double both ends back on themselves, using plenty of line. Use the braided line for tying. Take at least eight turns around the mono, pull tight and clip the ends.

The Improved Clinch Knot is used for tying flies, lures and hooks to monofilament lines or leaders. To tie the knot, thread the end of the line through the eye of the hook or swivel and make five or more turns around the standing part of the line. Then run the end between the eye and the first loop, and then back through the big loop. Hold the end and pull tight.

Tests by Dupont have shown that it is very important to make at least five turns around the standing part of the line when tying the Blood Knot and the Improved Clinch Knot in monofilament. Knot strength drops off sharply as the number of turns decreases below five.

Knots in monofilament should be pulled up slowly and tightly, not jerked into place as was necessary with gut leaders of an earlier era.

Above all, don't hesitate to retie your lure or leader frequently. Only a few seconds is required to make a new connection, and this can mean the difference between landing and losing that lunker.

Line and Leader Tests

One manufacturer's "10-pound test" line may be stronger than that of another. Most have a built-in safety factor which will give slightly more strength than the test listed on the package. With monofilament, particularly, line strength generally varies directly with line diameter, so govern your selection accordingly.

As opposed to the normal line, where the given test rating is the *minimum* breakload for the line, there are lines which are called "class" lines. These refer to the various classes established by the International Game Fishing Association (IGFA), and the test rating of a "class" line indicates the *maximum* breakload for that particular line. A 10-pound-test class line will not test more than 10 pounds, while a normal 10-pound-test line will not test below 10 pounds.

CHAPTER TWENTY-EIGHT

The Bass Fishing Boat

AFTER twenty years of searching I have found what I consider the best bass-fishing boat available. With it I can efficiently fish the majority of bass waters which can be fished with any other boat —with the pirogue or the cruiser. This boat is made of fiberglass, and has an inverted "W" bow design which scoops in air to help smooth out the bumps. It has a double bottom with floatation foamed in between. It is 14′9″ along the centerline, 54″ wide and weighs 280 pounds. It will handle a maximum of 40 horsepower on the stern, but I use a 20-hp outboard and get an honest 20-25 miles per hour, depending upon how clean the hull is. A faster rig is helpful at times, but this speed covers a lot of water and the decreased gasoline consumption is a decided advantage.

My boat has two seats plus a small deck up front. A third middle seat is optional, but I prefer to have the center area open. If it's necessary to accommodate a third fisherman, I place a low, folding chair in the middle, or just let him sit on an ice box.

I operate the boat from the forward seat, which requires remote controls for starting (electric starting outboard), gearshift, throttle and steering. The first three are positioned on the starboard side of the boat and, since they are common, need no further comment.

Author's ideal bass-fishing rig, which evolved after almost three decades of experimenting, is a 15-foot Terry Bass Boat made of fiberglass, with a 20-hp Johnson outboard on the stern and a Motor-Guide electric motor on the bow. Trailer is a heavy-duty Tee-Nee. The outfit is pulled by a four-wheel-drive Kaiser-Jeep Wagoneer which cruises in comfort at 60-75 mph.

The Terry is big enough to take quite a bit of rough water, to stand in safely while fishing, and to walk around in to stretch, yet it is small enough to be maneuverable. Complete bow controls give added convenience, efficiency and visibility.

Remote steering, on the other hand, usually involves a steering wheel, which is an abomination on a bass-fishing boat. Instead of a wheel, I use stick steering which is positioned on the port side of the boat for left-hand operation.

Stick steering is not common in most parts of the country, but has become very popular in my home area. Jim Dockery is the man who developed the Jim Stick several years ago, and in 1965 improved it with a geared version which is smoother, easier to operate, and which removes the effect of big outboard torque. For details about the Jim Stick write Dockery at Reeves Marine Center, 3210 Lakeshore Drive, Shreveport, Louisiana.

Why operate the boat from the bow? Visibility is tremendously improved. You can avoid obstructions which would not be possible to see from the stern seat. You never have a blind spot caused by a front-seat passenger, because there's never anyone in front of you. Also, when you stop the outboard and begin to fish, you're in the best fishing position there in the bow.

The Motor-Guide, an electric motor attached to the bow, is a great boon for the bass fisherman. Here it is shown in traveling position with shock cord in place to keep it from bumping during transportation.

To bring motor into operating position, motor shaft is lifted to vertical position and locked.

With a cord provided for the purpose, the motor is lowered into water.

Motor-Guide in position for use. One foot pedal controls all operations. Rocked slightly to the right, the pedal starts the motor; rocked forward or backward, the pedal guides the boat in any direction.

On the bow of my boat I have a Motor-Guide, one of the greatest boons to the bass fisherman ever invented. It is an electric motor which is controlled entirely with one foot pedal. Pressure of that one foot starts or stops the motor, and guides the boat in any direction—even backwards. This allows the fishermen to do more fishing in a specified time, to keep his lure in the water. With it he can position the boat properly to fish each area and keep it there as long as he chooses. He can fish more efficiently for longer periods of time because he is not tired from fighting a paddle, a particularly frustrating and fatiguing chore if the wind is blowing. The Motor-Guide is manufactured by the Herschede Hall Clock Company, Starkville, Mississippi.

Power for the electric starter on the outboard, and for the electric motor, is provided on my boat by a single 12-volt battery. I have it in a metal box with a battery charger, fastened to the floor between the stern seat and the transom. Each night when I end the fishing day I plug the charger in to the nearest outlet. I carry a 100-foot extension cord for this purpose. If you're out of reach of electricity, of course, better take an extra battery or use the one sparingly.

There's room behind that stern seat for a gasoline tank for the outboard, which frees the working area of the boat from tank or fuel line.

Screen-door holders keep rods neatly clipped to the inside of the boat.

Geared Jim Stick makes front-end steering easy and practical, eliminating steering wheel which often gets in the way of fishing.

The floor of the boat is *level*, and this is important. If it is slanted toward the middle all gear gravitates together with each bump. I like to stand up in the boat and fish from time to time. It gets the kinks out of your legs, and you can fish better because you can see better and have more freedom of action. If the floor of the boat isn't level, standing on it is tiring and your platform is much less stable. There is nothing wrong with standing in a boat to fish, despite all you may have heard, but you must have a boat in which it is safe to stand.

My boat is a Terry Bass Boat, built by Bass Boats Incorporated, P.O. Box 635, Hurst, Texas. Another similar boat is the Kingfisher. Also similar, and excellent fishing boats although not quite as comfortable, or as dry in a chop, are the Skeeter and Hustler.

This Terry will take a surprising amount of rough water. Fiberglass is not as noisy as aluminum, and requires less maintenance than does wood. My boat sits low in the water and is not affected by wind nearly as much as are many other designs and materials. It can be paddled or sculled easily.

I like a boat with lots of room in it, because I frequently carry lots of gear. That often includes three rods; two tackle boxes;

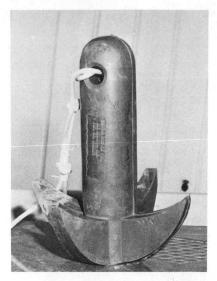

Padded boat seat eases the strain of long hours on a lake.

Two good anchors should be part of boat's equipment. This one, of metal covered with rubber, is effective and quiet.

another tackle box which I have fitted out as a camera case (waterproof, inconspicuous and handy); a Fish Lo-K-Tor; landing net; an aluminum box which holds such items as rain gear, jacket, extension cord for battery charger, sealed beam spotlight which plugs into battery box, a couple of extra "quick squeeze" life preservers, candy bars and other snacks, rain covers for the padded boat seats, extra length of line; and an ice box.

Always in the boat are life preserver cushions or jackets, a paddle and a small tool box (GI ammo box) which contains spare spark plugs, spark-plug wrench, pliers, screw driver and outboard-motor manual.

My boat is equipped with the best, padded, swivel boat seats I could find. There are several good brands available, but mine happen to be Scott Port-a-Fold, since I have found them to be extremely sturdy, to give excellent back support, and to be very comfortable.

I carry two anchors in my boat, and these are sometimes the most important fishing equipment an angler can have. Use the type best suited to the bottom where you fish. One of the nicest to use is made with an iron core covered with molded rubber.

Another useful aid is a 2- or 3-foot length of shock cord fastened to your boat near the seat. With it you can quickly tie the boat to stump or limb, which is sometimes more convenient than anchoring.

In my boat I built a rod rack along each side. Commercial rod holders are available, but the best are to be found at your nearby hardware store—the spring holders used for screen doors. Attached to the inner side of the boat, they will hold your rod handle firmly. A hook for the other end of the rod completes the setup.

My boat trailer is heavier than I need for just the boat, but it has the beef to support the boat when I'm using it for a luggage trailer. When we leave for the backwoods on a camping-fishing trip, tents, sleeping bags, cooking gear and fishing tackle often ride along in the boat. My trailer is a Tee-Nee Model 900, but there

Flat-bottomed johnboat, a popular craft for bass fishing, is suitable for small lakes, for streams, and for protected waters.

Light, durable aluminum boat or canoe is an excellent choice for the angler who wants to transport his rig atop his car.

are many good ones available. A poor trailer will frequently destroy a good boat in a short time.

Our family auto will tow my bass boat anywhere there are roads, and can launch it at many unimproved sites. My favorite tow vehicle, however, is our four-wheel-drive Kaiser-Jeep Wagoneer station wagon. With it I can get my boat and trailer to almost any lake or stream shore, and with the 4X in compound low I can launch and retrieve the boat in astoundingly difficult spots.

A four-wheel-drive tow vehicle is a decided advantage if you fish many lakes or streams where improved launching ramps are not available. There are a number of good ones on the market—Toyota, Scout, Bronco and Land Rover. I chose the Wagoneer because it is big enough to accommodate my family of five, and because it will cruise at 60 mph on the highways in comfort.

My favorite bass-fishing rig does have limitations, and by examining them we can explore the areas where other boats excel. First, there are backwoods areas where a vehicle can go but a trailer pulled along behind cannot. The twists and turns are too much. In this case a cartop boat is the answer, which to me is something that weighs considerably less than 280 pounds. In the cartop class are canoes, aluminum johnboats, the Penn Yan boats, light aluminum semi-V's and the like. I use them all on occasion.

There are times and places where it is necessary to transport a boat by hand a considerable distance overland. Portages from one drainage to another, from one lake to another, are common in such spots as Minnesota's Quetico-Superior, and here there is no substitute for the canoe. It packs a load well, paddles easily and can be portaged by one man. In parts of the South, the pirogue, made either of aluminum or marine plywood, takes the place of the canoe.

My Terry Bass Boat draws very little water, but even that is too much for floating some streams. On these the flat-bottomed johnboats are usually just right. A narrow creek boat is even better on the smaller creeks, particularly those which offer many obstacles.

The cruiser, or the big semi-V's, have an advantage in getting back home if foul weather arises while you're fishing. If the wind and waves get too severe I may have to run to the nearest bank and wait it out, while the bigger craft can plunge on through, but the fishing efficiency of my rig outweighs this consideration.

CHAPTER TWENTY-NINE

The Tackle Box

THE classic bass-fishing cartoon showed an angler in his boat, towing a raft on which his giant tackle box resides. It was funny then and it still is today—even more so. For the tackle "requirements" of bass fishermen continue to grow as the years pass. New lures appear on the scene and are musts, but then we can't discard the old favorites and leave them behind.

The behavior of a bass fisherman buying a tackle box is as predictable as the sun. When he buys his first outfit, "that little box over there in the corner will be fine." In a month he has found that the box must carry more than lures, so he buys a bigger one. In six months he repeats the process, rationalizing that his wife and son can use the other two. Within a year or two he is past the point of needing to rationalize, and continues his search for bigger and better boxes.

The moral is obvious! Buy a BIG tackle box to begin with. It will overflow soon enough, but in it you'll have room for the necessities of bass-fishing life. In a small one you do not.

Anglers who are addicted to plug casting have the biggest problem with tackle boxes, since many of the lures they use are big. Those who confine their tackle to spinning or spincast gear

245

reduce the needed size of their lure containers, and the fly fisherman has hardly any problem at all.

But the problem isn't that simple, because lures are only a part of what the well-equipped tackle box should contain. Here are some items which I found in mine: tightly rolled rain shirt with hood; insect repellent; roll of pressure-sensitive, plastic electrician's tape; tube of ointment to prevent sunburn; small flashlight; pair of polaroid glasses; fish-cleaning knife; miniature pair of binoculars; a Res-Q-Pak; a plug knocker; tube of cement; pair of Sargent fishing pliers; pair of regular pliers; screwdrivers; spark-plug wrench; a HooKouT, which is the best tool available for removing hooks or lures from deep within a bass's mouth; a beer-can opener; hook hone; small file; assorted shear pins; and a compact first-aid kit which includes aspirins, waterproof match box, compass, snakebite kit, small GI candle (excellent for starting fires or heating ferrules),

Tackle boxes come in a vast array of sizes, but the beginner invariably chooses one too small to cope with his growing lure supply.

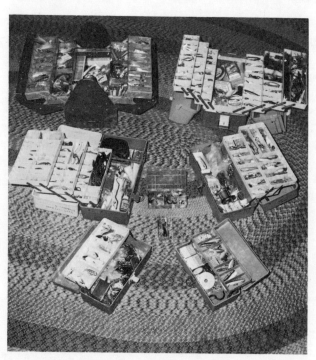

and band-aids; a De-Liar with which to weigh and measure fish; and a couple of candy bars.

Let's examine that array of gear. Some kind of rain gear should go along on every fishing trip you make. In the gear box of my regular fishing boat I carry a rain suit—pants and pullover jacket with hood, made of light, tough, completely waterproof nylon by Charles Ulmer, Inc., Sailmakers of City Island, N. Y.; but in my tackle box I also carry one of the fine rain shirts made by Hodgeman. It's a hooded pullover which reaches below the knees when you're standing. When you're seated in a boat it covers you completely.

Many trips have been ruined by a sudden shower which drove the angler from the lake when he should have been fishing. Frequently the rain will end within an hour, but by then the fisherman is often back at the dock, wet and disgusted, and reluctant to go back out. Another point is that immediately preceding and following rain the weather is cloudy. Light intensity is low, and that is when fishing is usually best. The angler who scoots for the dock at the approach of rain misses this prime time. If lightning is involved, of course, get off the lake.

The roll of tape has a thousand uses—replacing rod guides, fastening reel to rod, mending rips in rain gear or waders, etc. The same is true of the cement. The best I've found is Parla Klister Swedish Pearl Cement Formula #2.

The binoculars give me a great deal of enjoyment when I'm out fishing, in addition to being a helpful aid. I'm a bird watcher both for pleasure and for bass, for egrets, herons and gulls will often lead you to bass by leading to the forage fish the bass are after. On big waters the glasses keep me from doing a lot of unnecessary wandering. With them I can pick out landmarks on the far side of the lake and motor directly to the one I choose.

My plug knocker is a homemade hunk of lead cast in a pear-shape mold, with an eye on top for a cord and a clip through which to run my fishing line. Cheap, efficient plug knockers can be made from old, discarded spark plugs, just by bending the "gap" down over one end of a paper clip. In use, slip your line through the clip, drop the plug down to the lure, and jiggle it up and down. That will usually dislodge the plug but, if not, you haven't lost much other than your lure.

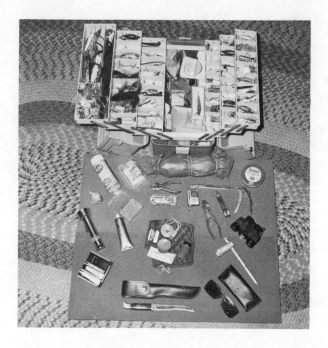

In addition to lures, author's tackle box holds a variety of useful gear: rain-shirt, Res-Q-Pak, insect repellent, plug knocker, flashlight, cement, fish knife, polaroid glasses, sparkplug wrench, binoculars, HookOut, tape, fishing pliers, shear pins, sun lotion, De-Liar, pliers, can opener, candy bar, and emergency kit with compass, snakebit kit, waterproof match box, candle, band-aids and aspirin.

The other items from my box are self-explanatory. In addition to them, I frequently carry a spare reel and a spare spool of line.

Materials and Design

Most tackle boxes marketed today are either of steel, aluminum or plastic. A few wooden boxes are available here and there. Aluminum is lighter than plastic, but the latter takes hard knocks better and isn't as noisy. Steel is stronger than aluminum, but heavier and will rust. I use aluminum and plastic boxes.

When choosing a box give particular attention to the fittings, to the hinges and the latches. They should be well made and rust-proof, for they are often the first points of a box to give trouble. I prefer a box with a lock, to discourage meddling and prevent theft of items in the box.

Except for size of the box itself, your most important consideration in the selection is the size and arrangement of the compartments in the trays of the box. Examine as wide a selection as you can, and try to visualize just what you'll be putting in those compartments. If you like to use big plug-casting lures, make sure the tackle box you choose has some compartments big enough for them. Many boxes do not.

If you confine your fishing to the use of small lures, usually identified as spinning size, get a box with many small compartments. Most of us use some of both and prefer a variety of compartment sizes. The depth of the area beneath the trays varies considerably. Select the arrangement which suits you best.

The size of the box, too, is up to you. We've said that your first ones will probably be too small, but just how big you care to go depends on factors which only you can evaluate. Hip-roof boxes are manufactured which have a dozen trays in them.

Depending upon the boat you normally use, it may be better for you to have two or three smaller boxes than one big one. I find it convenient, for instance, to use a separate, small box for my plastic-worm fishing material. It contains worms, hooks, sinkers, leadheads, jigs and jars of pork eel. Keep your plastic worms in a clear plastic bag, one for each color, and you'll keep your tackle box a lot neater.

Clean your tackle box out periodically. Most important, leave it open overnight after you've been fishing. Air circulates through it and evaporates any moisture which would rust hooks, knives and other metal items. A drop or two of oil on metal working parts, such as hinges and latches, will keep them in good condition.

CHAPTER THIRTY

Guides

F<small>OR</small> two years I owned and operated a fishing resort on a very good bass lake. From throughout the nation came fishermen to try their luck, and when they called or wrote for reservations I always asked, "Do you want to reserve a guide?" Each time I anxiously awaited their answer.

Those who did engage the services of a guide, at least for the first day or two of their stay, usually caught some bass. A great majority of those who did not, if they were fishing the lake for the first time, did not catch bass. It is not surprising that I strongly recommended a "yes" answer, since nothing was as apt to make a guest shorten his visit as two or three fishless days.

Scenery, weather, companionship, lodging and food—all can be superb, but if the object of a trip is to bass fish there should be a few bass involved.

It is true that the lake in question is unusually difficult for a stranger to cope with, but every body of bass water tends to exact its toll on the first-time angler. Using a guide for the first session or two is often a most economical move.

Guide fees vary widely in different areas, from as little as $5 or $10 a day to as much as $25 or $35 a day. The higher figures often

include use of a boat and motor, but sometimes do not. Sometimes
there are half-price fees for an afternoon of fishing, and this is a
good bet if you're on a budget yet need to learn something about
the lake. The half-price rate is usually not available for morning
fishing, since that would keep the guide from getting an all-day
job.

Remember, first of all, that your guide is not a miracle man. No
matter how good he is, he cannot produce instant bass on demand.
His ratio of success to failure will be many times as good as that of
strangers in the area, but there will still be days when he can't
"buy" a bite. Bass are really magicians. They can turn men into
monkeys in the wink of an eye, and that includes fishing guides.

Now, you have decided to hire a guide, which is most often done
through the dock operator at the resort where you'll fish. The first
thing you should do is to firmly establish exactly what the guide
fee is, what it includes (is boat and motor extra?), and just what
constitutes a "day."

A "day" for some guides begins at daylight and ends when the
light is gone, if the customer can stand that much fishing. For
others it may be eight hours. For some it may be until you catch
a limit of bass, or until you and he together catch one limit of bass.
Some guides don't care to greet the sunrise and won't leave the
dock until after a daylight breakfast.

The point is to make sure that you and he understand each other.
If his specifications don't suit you, and you can't prevail upon
him to change them, don't use him.

Remember that a boat paddler is not necessarily a fishing guide.
If you want a boat paddler, tell the dock operator that's what you
want. If you want a good fishing guide, however, impress on the
dock operator that you want a guide and not just a paddler. Many
fishing camps have a habit of foisting off on unsuspecting visitors,
particularly those who arrive without notice or reservation, anybody
who can travel the lake without getting lost.

After you have engaged the guide, ask him what lures the bass
are hitting. If you haven't got what he recommends, and it's available, buy it. Your plugs may catch as many bass, but you're being
pennywise and pound foolish if you chance it.

While you're afloat the guide's time is your time. You can fish any way *you* choose and where *you* choose and when *you* choose, but in doing so you defeat the purpose of hiring a guide. To get the most from his services, fish when, where and how *he* recommends. If you try it his way for a reasonable length of time without success, don't be afraid to suggest something else. Guides aren't infallible, and most welcome the chance to learn something from a client. It's always possible that you have brought with you a lure or technique which will prove a killer on that particular occasion.

Should your guide fish? That depends entirely upon you. Most guides like to fish—that's often why they got into the business, but some do not. If you prefer that he doesn't, that's your prerogative for you're paying for his time. But you could be defeating your chances of filling a stringer. With two of you experimenting your chances increase for "establishing the pattern." Once you've discovered what the bass are hitting, and where and how, you can do all the fishing if you like. Until then, if the guide can fish and still handle the boat, and if the law doesn't prevent him from fishing, I recommend that you let him. If you do, remember that some guides will insist that their day is completed when a limit of bass is boated, regardless of who catches them. If you find yourself afloat with one of these, you didn't check carefully enough before hiring him.

The best guides want *you* to catch bass. They will want to fish until the pattern is established, until the right recipe for the day is found, but then they will sit back and let you take over. If not, don't be timid about insisting that they do.

If you are a good bass fisherman, you pay a fishing guide primarily for his knowledge of the waters. He shortens the time required for you to find the fish, because he already knows where they should be. If you're an average bass fisherman, you're paying him for knowing the waters, but also for establishing the pattern for you.

In either case, if you plan to use a guide each day you fish the lake, you can just have fun and have at it. If you are just using a guide for a day or two, however, to get your feet on the ground, to learn enough about this new lake so that you can go it alone, then pay attention. Observe everything your guide does. When you leave the boat dock watch where you're going, making mental notes which will help you return to the same spots later when you're alone. If you have your head buried in the task of rigging your tackle, you will miss the important landmarks that will help you later.

Paying close attention requires effort. If you are an average bass fisherman, and want to get better, observe everything your guide does. Absorb where he takes you, what lures he fishes, how he rigs them, and how he fishes them. You have a first-class bass fishing instructor in the boat with you, so take advantage of the opportunity. The good bass fisherman will do most of this instinctively, for odds are that he became good by doing so.

Some of the best guides I've had around the country have been unpaid nonprofessionals, the local fishermen who have taken me under their wing, who have shared their favorite fishing holes, and who have revealed to me their secrets of bass fishing. You can find them in service stations and grocery stores, in restaurants and in sporting goods stores, at bait stands and barber shops, and at fishing resorts. How do you find them? By being friendly, by being interested, by inviting help and suggestions. These men are on their home grounds and you're a stranger. Wait for them to come to you and you wait a long time.

Above all, never pass on to others the exact locations of your host's favorite spots unless you have his permission to do so. If you do you're violating a trust, an unwritten code which is firm and inflexible.

Index

A

Abu-Reflex plug, 98
Adcock, Bill, 37 ff., 45, 101, 102
Agricultural Experimental Station, 33
Alabama, smallmouth bass in, 21
    spotted bass in, 23
Al Foss Shimmy Wiggler lure, 91
Allatoona Lake, Georgia, 23
Arbogast, Fred, 91–2
Arizona, bottom bumping, 61
Arkansas, big bass in, 150
    Buffalo River, overfishing in, 28
    smallmouth bass in, 21
    spotted bass in, 23

B

Baits, acceptability, 86
    artificial, 84 ff.
    plastic, soft, 86
    for big bass, 148
    fishing technique with, 79 ff.
    natural, 78 ff.
    capturing with Fish Lo-K-Tor, 78
    eels, 83
    pork, 86
    shrimp, 83
    see also Lures
Bang O Lure buoyant lure, 107
"Bass and Bluegills, Managing Farm Fishponds for," 31
Bass bug, 88
    see also Lures
Bass, in bunches, 54 ff.
Bass Buster jig, 117
Bass (fishing)
    better, pointers on, 151
    big (lunkers), 143 ff.
    big catches of, 150
    care in manipulating, 128
    depth, 144
    Florida, technique, 80
    locating, 144
    lures for, 144–5, 148
    season, 145

    spinning for, 217–18
    world's biggest caught, 144
    bigger catches, 54 ff.
    establishing pattern, 51–3
    frequency, value of, 155, 157–8, 159
    notebook, use of, 159
    boat and equipment for, 235 ff.
    boating the, 131–6
    bottom bumping for, 56
    bottom hugging, 56 ff.
    bottom structures favoring, 168
    clustering around lure, 66–7
    fly casting, 187 ff.
    fly fishing, equipment and technique, 187 ff.
    handling the catch, 175 ff.
    cleaning, 176, 180
    cookery, 181–2
    freezing, 180
    keeping it fresh, 175–6
    storage, 180
    lines, leaders and knots for, 225 ff.
    locating, 37–50
    lure, reactions to, 16
    moon phases, relation to, 171–2
    night, 73 ff.
    pattern, establishing, 51 ff.
    plug casting, equipment and technique, 201 ff.
    productivity, increase and decrease, 161 ff.
    hot lakes, 161–4
    schooling, 54 ff.
    shad as clues in, 170
    skittering, 137 ff.
    spincasting, 211–13, 219 ff.
    spinning, 211 ff.
    tackle box for, 245 ff.
    techniques in
    boating, 131–6
    the cast, 121–3
    the fight, 127–31
    the retrieve, 123–6
    the strike, 126–7
    wading, 65 ff.
    water fluctuations, reaction to, 17–18
    weather affecting, 165 ff.

W

Water conditions
  depth correlation, 168
  flow favoring concentrations, 54–5
  temperature measuring, 166
Wading
  gear
  clothing and waders, 68–9
  inner tube rig, 71
  lures, 66, 69
  net, 69
  "ski" belt, 71
  in overflows, 66
  safety, 71–2
  in spring shallows, 65 ff.
Waterdog lure, 101
Weather conditions
  barometric pressure, 172
  cloud cover, 172–3, 247
  foul, boats for, 244
  gear for, 173, 240, 247
  lightning, 247
  rain, 172
  temperature, reactions of bass to, 166
  wind, force and direction, 169
  worm holes, fishing, in hot or cold, 120
Weber's Mr. Champ spoon, 91
Welch, Sam, 118, 150
Whiskerbug lure, 91
White River, Ark., 23, 33

Whitmore Lake, Mich., 24
Whopper Stopper lure, 101, 107
Wilcox, Robert H., *quoted*, 25
Wilder, B. F., 88
Wilder-Dilg fly, 88
Wilder's Discovery, 88
Wilder's Minnow, 88
Wildlife
  activity periods for, 170–2
  see also Moon
  management, principle of, 26
  research on conservation of, 32 ff.
Wilson Dam, Ala., 80
Wilson Lake, Ala., 21
Wind conditions, 169–70
Wisconsin, creel limits, 28
Witt, Bob, 17
Wooden Classics lures, 96
Wooly Worm, 90
Worden, Frank G., 96
Worms
  for big bass, 148, 149
  in overflow waters, 66
  plastic, 63, 77, 90, 110 ff.
  worm holes, 120
Wyoming, creel limits, 28

Z

Zane Grey lure, 88
Zaragossa stickplug, 106
Zara Spook stickplug, 106, 149